Bards Annual 2021

The Annual Publication of The Bards Initiative

Bards Initiative

James P. Wagner (Ishwa)—Editor, Compiler

Nick Hale—Submissions Editor, Compiler

Marc Rosen—Associate Editor

J R Turek—Associate Editor

Cover Art: Vincent (VinVulpis) Brancato

Layout Design: James P. Wagner (Ishwa)

Bards Annual 2021

Copyright © 2021 by Bards Initiative

www.localgemspoetrypress.com

Dedicated to all the poets past and present on Long Island!

Foreword

This is the eleventh year of Bards Annual. Last year for our 10th anniversary we were forced to handle things much differently than we normally did because of the Global Pandemic restricting how many people could be in a room at a time. Nevertheless, we made it work.

The world of Covid hit the poetry communities like it hit everything else. While virtual events have sprung up to fill the void, there is nothing that will ever quite replace the energy, connection and community of in-person live events. We knew this long before Covid—in a world where technology advances exponentially every year, people still gathered for live concerts, seminars, conventions and other in-person events despite the fact, that so much, theoretically, could be delivered virtually.

Having done virtual seminars and presentations long before Covid hit, we were not ignorant of this fact, and the world soon learned just how much we could do without being in-person, but, for some things, the virtual just doesn't cut it. Poetry readings are a great example of this.

Why? Because poetry is, more than anything about human connection, reflection, and introspection. Some of which you can do in private while reading a book or watching a video or hearing a recording—but some of it comes from the energy you collect from everyone at a live event that just doesn't translate well without being there.

With the worst of Covid (hopefully) behind us, and things returning to relative normalcy, one thing is obvious; the Pandemic left its mark on the world. And one of the things that happened, sadly for the poetry community, is many of the venues that used to host our events have shuttered permanently.

Outdoor events, parking lot readings, and flash mob poetry in parks were all seasonal or temporary solutions that helped the giant gap, but it became very obvious that the community needed a place to call its own again.

Despite all the troubles this year, we pressed forward on a dream that we've had for over a decade, and we opened "The Dog-Eared Bard's Book Shop" in East Northport.

The place is a haven for used, antiquarian and independent books. But more importantly, it is a place for consistent, live, in-person poetry readings for those eager to get out and connect with people again. At the time of this writing we have had over half-a-dozen events in the place, and aim to have many more.

We view this push into the next level as the Bards Initiative as a whole taking a jump into further legitimacy. There are plenty of other groups and organizations that have establishments of their own, Lodges, Knights of Columbus, Motorcycle Clubs, etc. Why not poets?

Now, the Long Island poetry scene has at least one place we can call our home, hopefully for many years to come. And readings and workshops are finding a way to come back in creative new ways as well. We are a very resilient and steadfast group, us poets. And we will always find ways to work on and share our craft as we have done for thousands of years.

~ James P. Wagner (Ishwa)

Table of Contents

Lloyd Abrams

a lamentation for the trees

maples and tupelos
sassafras and sycamores
spruces and elms
come tumbling down
in tropical storms and blizzards
in nor'easters and hurricanes
… our wooded neighborhood
gets depleted by nature's vagaries
mournful though understandable

but also by the cruel and oblivious
who absolutely *need* that inground pool
who abhor those messy herons
nesting above their driveways
who despise the boisterous crows
meeting late every afternoon
who are terrified that the next weather event
might – just might – bring down
onto their manicured lawns
a perfectly healthy
century-old oak

they don't or can't realize
that their malicious transgression
affects not only themselves
but every single one of us

we are all inalterably diminished

1

Sharon Anderson

Spare

Night was falling, the room was in shadow,
but Mom wouldn't light the lamps
until it was absolutely necessary,
and we could still see well enough to eat.

Supper was a feast that evening.
My brother had caught a rabbit,
so the "stew" that night
actually contained meat.

We held hands around the table,
bowed our heads, said grace.
I added my own silent prayer
that there might be eggs for breakfast.

We had never been rich,
but this year was particularly bad.
A drought claimed most of our crops,
and Dad was laid off from the mill.

We all survived, and things got better.
Dad found a job, the drought ended.
Mom turned the lamps on at dusk,
and always served meat for supper.

But I never forgot that bleak, spare year,
and the fear I felt in my heart.
Never forgot those times when
my prayers included a plea for eggs.

William H. Balzac

Gathering

There is,
As I gather each object
Which has accumulated
Within this House,
The feeling
That everything we've carried
Within our memory
Shall be precious:
Something which will never
Fully be articulated in Words,
But with Time
Shall be taken in
By somebody.

Christine Barbour

Beneath the Dirt

for my 2nd Great Grandfather: Anson Ferguson b. 1835 –d. 1902

Who savors you more than us, the unfallen, long after we've forgotten
the fallen beneath?   Li-Young Lee

As you lay beneath the dirt
for more than a century,
twigs and leaves have scattered
around your funeral pyre
that has never been burned
or wet with anyone's tears.

Someone must have planted
this Japanese Maple tree
next to your headstone
soon after you passed
as a talisman and to shelter you
from Nature's elements,
but Nature is strong
and the sun and storms
have weathered your name
from the granite marker --
all that remains is a plot number
written on a scrap of paper
and a copy of the cemetery's map
handed to me by the curator
at the front gate.

I am happy that we have found
one another back through Time.
I lay white lilies on your grave,
better suited to the metaphor of life and
place a stone atop your pillar to show
that stones and souls endure.
I am amazed that we are family: blood,
DNA above and below both worlds.

Patricia Z. Beach

A View During My Pandemic Stroll

I walk during the pandemic
It stills my restless mind
Past the numbing sameness of suburbia
One house alone stands out
Its numbers obscured by time
Appearing frozen, no car sits in the driveway
Rather an abandoned RV, sinks in its tracks
Edged out by weeds
A gas canister rests as witness
The lawn is faded and unkempt
The shutters uneven, windows unbalanced
Leaders pull away from the exposed roof
I imagine what promise this house once held
And almost hear children's laughter from a gentler time
Wonder is someone inside quietly watching, waiting
For our world to return to normal
I pass by unnoticed

Joe Beck

People Flowers

the loudest in the room
is always the last to bloom
forget the class president
we all know what
happens to the popular vote
it's the quiet one
in the back who
watches the parade
tornado mouths wreck
thoughtful people build
fertile, fecund
minds are the patient soil
to grow stunning blooms
in renewable,
sustainable
greenhouses
the weakest scream
the strongest dream
blooms are the open,
strongest minds
letting worker bees
freely cross-pollinate
ideas for the
whole hive,
honey

Antonio Bellia (Madly Loved)

I Am

I have traced
My origins,
Gone back and
Crossed the dark
Behind
Not remembrance.

I dared to look
Behind the forming
Time.
I saw past my
Mother's womb.

I was not blinded
By the splendor.
I looked with eyes closed.

I saw the splendor
That illuminates,
The light
That crumbles
The walls of darkness,
An expanding blaze
That like a ripple
Moving outward,
Dispelled gloom
With glare,

Broadcasting stars,
Planets, and living things.

I saw a flash
Of that light
Becoming my soul.

Robyn Bellospirito

Boardwalk to the Sea

Boardwalk to the sea
against all the wishes of the whispering trees
I walk the board unto the sea
waves clapping at my arrival
wind playing roughly with my hair
taking bits and wisps of sand in swirls
high into the air
in this wild place
where the Great Mother reminds us
of what it was like
to be born

Selina Benson

Thoughts About Thoughts

Yesterday I had a thought, I thought I'd need to keep.
I thought about it everyday and dreamt it in my sleep.
And then I had another thought, I thought I'd hold that too.
It wasn't like the other thought, this thought was something new.
And then a third, a fourth a fifth, eleven, twelve thoughts more.
Like grains of sand upon a beach, I soon had thoughts galore.
Soon thoughts were racing in my mind, they bounced round to and fro.
Though there was little space for more, I let not one thought go.
I started losing track of them. I found I couldn't guess.
Which was the thought that I thought first?
Which thought had I thought best?
I thought my thoughts were my best part. I thought, one just won't do.
But as I think about my thoughts, I didn't think it through.
I kept my thought unto myself, but seems it was for naught.
I wish someone would offer me, a penny for my thoughts

Thérèse M. Craine Bertsch

I Feel a Haunting

#1 The Meeting
In that room I knew there way
Yes
It is true you know, that it was you.
And, who knows in the underground of genes or in the DNA
if we were meant to be.

I didn't ask, somehow I knew the way
I didn't ask, your presence really was all you had to say. Yes
In that room I knew the way.

As life unfolds and multiplies with ripening fruit and other ways
And others too, yes and it all began with you.
Well, is that so? I do not know.

#2 The Grieving
I feel a haunting now within my bones which words cannot describe
This hollowness cannot be filled like dying while alive.

I'm traveling just now back to home, to make a home and passing bye
what it is we never owned, as no one ever does
but then, I wear that remnant in my flesh from all we've ever been.

And this is life and this is love
Our story never ends
Bejeweled in diamonds on I go, but never to pretend
Now, when I feel within may bones a call to count the loss
I enter in just as in birth then sail for other shores.

#3 Paradise Unfolds
It's paradise my head cried out in melancholy tone
Not in embraces from a love however much it's grown.
Withdrawing speedily from that shame at which remembering is aimed
When I recalled that blessed night, I blessed the night I blessed the light
Which never was too far from home.

My body met with destiny, my body wet from love of you
A wondrous love, yes - and then, from every portal of my being,
and one glorious risk now taken, we were just one.

My heart now breaking in reply sings out to heaven with a sigh.
It was not a taste of love forsaken nor was it just a love mistaken
But of unending love awakening.

Lorene Vorbach Bossong

Playing it Safe

spring terrifies me
all those tiny seeds poking up
with so much promise
how naïvely nature ventures out
ignoring the survival of the fittest rules
such audacity to think that your seed
will survive?
as if?

I'd rather lie dormant under winter ice
nestled in the earth
oblivious of my
fragility

Michael Brozinsky

Thanks all for liking my photos

I take my photos in auto mode
and results are in my humble abode
A good photographer can see my limitations
But setting suns are my salvations
A law of averages photog am
When I fail at least I try
My camera is not very expensive
Glad my results are sometimes pensive
I know not of aperture priority
And so, I am not an authority
I don't know what an F stop is
But I do love my country tis
Compliments of friends make me feel fine
And keeps me posting shots online

Rich Buley-Neumar

The World Changed

The world changed because everyone thought it should.
Everyone thought it should because they finally heard the truth.

They finally heard the truth because millions would not stay silent.
Millions would not stay silent because they learned what was true.

They learned what was true because thousands stood up.
Thousands stood up because they were inspired.

They were inspired because dozens told their stories.
Dozens told their stories because they found they were not alone.

They found they were not alone because one person had the courage to speak out.
That one person who had the courage to speak out was You.

So you see, my darling: You changed the world.

Alice Byrne

Cellphones dropped

I have so much more and embrace with love ,awareness.
Oh my life in the cave of awareness .
Without seeing I see so much more.
Dark space not so dark after all.
A different kind of seeing.
I feel the walls of the cave smooth here and rough over there.
No need to see just touch and smell.
I move my nose nearer the surface.
I smell the surface.Okay it's safe.
And my sixth sense brings news from outside the cave.
Grateful for all the awareness darkness brings.

Louisa Calio

Aunt Clara

Like Iphigenia, you were sacrificed to the winds of war
no less devastating than the battles of Troy
were these family conflicts.
Wasn't Agamemnon brother to Menelaus
and didn't he choose to murder his daughter
to serve his brother's needs and retrieve Helen?

Then why were we surprised you were sacrificed?
Perhaps because it was your mother
who gave her only daughter away
in service to her brothers.
Your poor mother
had lost both legs in her own battle with diabetes
and made hand sewn gloves
from her wheelchair in the basement
of your house in Brooklyn on 5th street.
I heard stories about how strong she was,
the woman who supported five children from home
while her husband, a dandy, roamed and cavorted.
Were you the price of your mother's courage?

The wars are over now.
We bury you today after 8 years of battling Alzheimer's
a disease that struck you like the Gorgon's glance,
turning you to stone, leaving you expressionless and silent.

You had worked so long, hard and joylessly at life
Needlessly to please those brothers
who barely noticed your sacrifice
They were used to your servitude
and though you married well you didn't spend
a dollar on yourself with ease.

My unforgettable childhood memory of you
was at four, when you arrived at our backyard party
and grabbed my arm hard before saying,
 "What are you so happy about?
It's not your birthday!"
The words struck like a slap, a thunderclap
you could do that.

That was then
Now I've appointed myself Electra on your behalf
 to speak for you an uneasy task
Who can judge a life?
The priest asked
calling you Martha for your meticulous work at home.
But I say Iphigenia,
Iphigenia sacrificed to the winds of the war
Italian immigrants faced.

Carlo Frank Calo

Salty Droplets

The tears come easy and always with purpose,
the drops blurring the things I should see.
They fall slowly, searching for answers,
to questions known only by me.

Sixty-year-old black and whites,
a time machine on paper.
Memories brought back to life,
breaking through the vapor.

The joy of life, it battles too,
chased by heartaches and remorse.
The wounds still bleed, the healing slow,
but healing takes its course.

Births and deaths are not the issue,
it's what's between that matters.
Answers to questions known only by me,
questions now blissfully shattered.

Lee grace Cannella

Paumanok Crossing

Remembering:
Carol, Barbara, Linda and Eileen

Dawn is fragile when she opens her eyes
to lift the night and welcome the sky.
The warming earth softens for seeding...
winter slowly ebbing away.

Island waters brush the shores
awakening bays and inlet streams,
salty air hovers over the bay
while inland fields are turning green.

Then, without warning,
a sudden storm, a virus death
shrouded the earth and its people.

Paumanok crossing
an everyday walk for so many:

My blond-headed friend
died alone under
a darkened sky.

Another's dancing feet
stepping into eternity
Unfettered...

22

A woman aglow,
held onto the light,
leading her home.

Smiling Irish eyes,
finding peace
in heaven's green.

So much suffering...
so many lonely deaths
buried in the land.

My island weeps
touching edging waters
with memory.

Waves crashing the beach
etching their names
on bone-white seashells
scattered in the sand.

LynneRose Cannon

Who knew you would be right?

once I thought I would be alone
and you said we should go
to that cartoon festival
down in the Village
and I thought no
but we did

I said, oh horrors, no minivan
but you said please
and we traveled
and the kids
sang along
with us.

I said if you turn into your father
and I turn into my mother
this could be terrible
but here we are
and we are
still us,
my love.

Gloria Cassandra-Jainchill

How Do I Know God?

How, oh God, do I know if you love me?
How God, do I see Your blessings for me?
How God, do I walk in the path You have set?
How God, do I rest in Your Love and the glow of Your rainbow?

Sit still My child,
Rest and walk with Me a while,
Feel My Presence,
In the beauty of fall's fragrance.

Colors orange red brown with sky blue,
Are part of the rainbow I created for you,
A taste, a smell, a small glimpse,
Of the beauty and love of My Presence.

I move the cool autumn wind,
Leaves fly everywhere in the air.
I listen, I see your pain and fears,
Holy Spirit tastes and dries your tears.

Be still My child,
Rest for a while,
As I rock you in My lap, hold you in My arms,
With your face snuggled against My Heart.

Cate Chirico

Indian Summer

I'm light as a feather,
this Indian summer weather
sunny as June warm as July
I feel I could fly into the glow of
the full moon's coming.
You make me smile
you're a brand new day ,
there are no rules
to this game we play
I just love you that's for sure.
I'm a bird on the wing singing ,
I'm the bell of the Dharma ringing,
hear my song ,come along,
I've known you from the beginning.

Jasmine Choi

I Need to Believe

I need to believe...
That man may be bold or blind but not evil.

I need to believe...
That when I am angry or fearful people aren't playing tricks with my mind.

I need to believe...
That life is a sacrifice and that sacrifice means everything to Christ.

I need to believe...
That truth will reign one day in the eyes of man.

I need to believe...
a vision is possible.

I need to believe...
that man and beast will play and prance in the desert..

Anne Coen

The Persistence of Memory

calendar lines disappear,
special occasions written in invisible ink
deadlines become irrelevant
there are no holidays
nothing to celebrate,
nothing to look forward to
one day bleeds into the next
a relentless cycle of
wash, rinse, repeat
nothing is familiar
in this strange land
we walk past trees
draped with melting clocks,
the persistence of memory
clinging to our clothes like smoke
life is an abstract painting

Joseph Coen

Wild Geese

Alarm unseen, unheard spreading everywhere
With a ruffle and flutter mounting to the air
Black specks dot the blue canvas
Long lines honking across the sky
Circling in a broad arc
Doubling back to settle once again
Only ripples disturb the pond

Jamie Ann Colangelo

The Baker's Dozen

A motley crew, they were
Gathered in from all walks
Businessmen, zealots, fishermen
Many educated, others not
Personalities varied from
Impeccably polished to
The rough and gruff
Yet, each one with a purpose
To fulfill the Baker's will

Everywhere the Baker went
They followed, watching,
Learning, questioning,
Being transformed by
His ways, thoughts,
Inspiration and love
Calling forth their
Greatness to step out
And transform the world

Wherever they traveled
The supernatural was
Brought forth in the natural
Miracles, signs, abounded
The sick healed, dead arose
Life restored to abundance
Encouraging others to

Rise up and step into
Who they were called to be

The Baker, used the least
Of these, a small boy,
A meager lunch of
Two fish and five loaves
Offered, through trust and sacrifice
Blessed, broke, multiplied and
Fed the multitudes,
5000 men and families to
Overflow of 12 large baskets

The Baker, is calling you
Arise, bring forth all
He's given to you
Transform the world by love
Lift up another
Give of what you have
Help raise up a brother,
Sister, one less fortunate,
To live an abundant life

Lorraine Conlin

On Eighth Street

I remember the days
and nights spent on 8th Street
before war took you away …

I remember rummaging through antiques
I Want to Hold Your Hand,
playing in every store.
We were so in love, always holding hands

I often stop and think about
that night outside the 8th Street Cinema
humming *Samba Saravah*
the theme from *A Man and A Woman.*
It was Thursday, April 4th
our song and dance ended with news
Martin Luther King was dead.

We embraced strangers
sobbed and cried
washed down bitter tears
with an *Orange Julius* we bought
next door to *Azuma*
Patchouli incense crept into night
Black lights, Day-Glo green and orange
a toke of reality on psychedelic 8th Street

32

We got lost
never found our way
but I know
I will never lose affection
for all these things
that came before …

Nancy Connolly

He'll make me feel good for a while.
I'll fly.
Like a clay pigeon.

Shakira Croce

Lullaby

When people ask me how I am,
I say "OK," but really I'm surprised by how
the bleeding began again so soon.
I tell them it feels good
sipping coffee, looking out
at the tangled mass
of branches between my window and the lake.
One day I will think back to all those laps
around Prospect Park,
rattles lost in the Long Meadow.
That toothless smile appears on cue.
Is it just a reflex?
There are worse things than a duplicate organ
steadily swelling in your gut.
My cherry blossom's pale weeping
weighs heavy on the steps.
I blame it on hormones or
the kind of love only a mother has for her son.
The grin turns to a grimace.
All I'm saying is that I thought
we would have a few more
good years. Petals clump
together, damp and brown.
Hush now love, I am here in your
ever-expanding sight.

Victoria Crosby

The Broken Pieces

When you feel like you are broken
into little pieces, don't despair,
for there are many different methods of repair.
A mosaic is made from many shards of broken china,
which are put together to make art so unique
that is even finer than the broken dishes of which I speak.

It is our friends who are the glue
that help us to
mend the broken pieces.

This is a story I've been told,
the Japanese put broken things together
and cover the cracks with precious gold,
then the broken item is more valuable than before.
So when life sends you reeling to the floor
remember this, and remember too
that something far more precious than gold is you.

It is our families who are the glue
to help us to
mend the broken pieces.

So don't blame yourself when life breaks your heart,
don't fall apart, but put those pieces together
like a mirrored disco ball, and shimmer and shine
until life returns the favor, and treats you just fine!

It is our faith that is the glue
that helps us to
mend the broken pieces.

Michele Cuomo

Communion

I stand by the shoreline watching the waves.
I stare forever and still do not understand
The physics of them.
I walk into the sea and submit to it
bowing down so as not to feel its rage
its animation and industry
its refusal to be still. It has a character--
I know why we thought it was a god once.
An ungainly angel, or rather, an egret
glides above and in that moment I will
also submit to views on reincarnation
if I could come back and swoop above the sea
for a time. Are egrets preyed upon
or do they die peaceful deaths?
Do they surrender to the sea
and let the sharks consume them
like Holy Communion wafers?
I will probably come back as an anhinga
instead stretching my feathers thin
reaching, straining for more. For more.

Paula Curci

I am a Poem

I am not a tabloid
I am a poem
a living breathing
carbon unit
beating

I am not editorial news
but a life story
of alternating text
A character with depth
rewriting

I am not a graphic novel
but a set of leather-bound
cherished on a shelf
to be opened with permission
for reading

I am not entertainment
a barrage of false narratives
for someone to create
so, it has a second go at
breaking

So, please stop telling me
What you think I am.
I AM... A POEM.

Megan Dausch

Egg

I roll an egg between my palms.
Still sheathed in
warmth from its journey in the bubbling water.
Dyes lined up on the table. A horizon of potential
ready to transform shells
into canvases.

Each moment
 an egg.
Full, waiting.
Liquid possibility.

I want to crack the shell of time.
Feel the power of my fingers
as they shatter the shell into shards.
Sometimes, I want to firmly cleave moments
apart, so the fragile core remains
whole and undisturbed.
Some moments I want to hard boil,
so I can cleanly dissect their meaning.
Some I wish to fold
into a batter so that they become
absorbed into something larger than themselves.
Some I wish I could scramble,
so I can't tease them apart.

Some moments blend into the background.
Some are the structure
that holds everything together.
Some I wish
to put back into the carton.
But each one contains
the building blocks of life.

Max Dawson

Pendulum Clocks

Galileo began the building blocks
Of the concept of pendulum clocks
His beginnings of this idea date
Back to the year, 1588
In the Cathedral of Pisa he observed one thing
He watched as a suspended lamp did swing
To draw this very concept he tried
And he completed it just before he died
It was Christiaan Huygens who found a way
To make clocks accurate to near one minute each day
Through math and physical analyses of how a clock ticks
Huygens invented his first pendulum clock in 1656
Huygens then patented his idea quite soon
In 1657, on the sixteenth of June

Jeanne D'Brant

Johnny

Paris, waiting to sight your silver bird in a flight pattern over Orly
Hotel charm and a bottle of Dom
wrought iron balconies and smoky bar banquettes
Stealing silently down the hallway to your room at 2am

We met in London, in a garden in June
You stood stately in uniform among the roses
Your captain's bars proudly gracing your shoulders
Your face and hands were my grandfather's
Like him, you were a son of the Deep South

Just one night, baby
It wasn't ever to be more
But what a curious thrill to make it with your grandfather's ghost
Twenty years down the line in the deep dark of printemps in Paris

Debbie De Louise

We All Lost Something During the Pandemic

(in memory of my friend, Clare)

We all lost something dear
during the pandemic.
I lost my friend Clare.
It wasn't fair.

She was kind,
funny, and sweet,
the nicest lady you could meet.

She loved cats,
attended church,
believed in prayer.
I can't believe she's no longer here.

We all missed so many things
during the pandemic.
I miss her smile,
her crazy stories.
It wasn't fair
that I lost Clare.

She had diabetes
and other conditions,
caught COVID
and died last spring.

Her sister called with the news.
It was the saddest thing.

All I have left
are the texts and birthday cards she sent
and the memories we shared.
I wish she was still here.
It's not fair.

A year has gone by
and the disease still spreads
despite shots, masks, and other measures.

We all want it to end
not to lose more family and friends.
To travel and socialize
not live in fear and anxiety.

We all lost so much
from the pandemic.
I lost my friend Clare.
It's not fair.

Sharon Dua

Never Again

Utterly destroyed
Never been hurt like this before
How did we get here
I'll tell you how
I opened my heart to you
I took a chance
You ran with it
Like a kite flying high in the sky
Then letting it go
When you raised it enough
Then pulled the wind from
Underneath
I slowly fell to the ground
But felt as if there was no bottom
Sitting later on a carousel
Spinning around and round
I raised my hands asking why
It didn't see it coming
I thought you loved me
Why , I Say
What , I Say
How, I Say
Your eyes look different now
Or did they always look that way
And I was just too blind to see
Felt the fog set in,
I knew it was time to leave

Why, I Say
What, I Say
How, I Say
I close my eyes
Stand my right foot forward
Hands reaching for the answer
That is never to be found
I stand straight up
Open my eyes
Never to look back
To be pulled
Where I did not belong
Never to say it again
Why, I once said
What, I once said
How, I once said
Never to look back
And I never did.

Michael Duff

Sixty

Life blusters away like dry leaves scuttling along the pavement:
a scattering and osseous scratch and rush.
What once was whirling and dancing,
meandering, an avid sweep
beside broad banks amid verdant hills
has found a hard channel between high walls;
too straight, gushing too swift and overwhelming, the surge,
darkening sky, enclosing bulwark
driving the flood, the deluge drowning all,
squeezed tighter, faster,
straight, inevitable as doctor's bills;
a spillway stretching inexorably
into the tumble and lurid expanse
that looms over human minds, now come into view.

Too many of life's joys reside in youth.

Madelyn Edelson

A Quiet Passion (The Life Of Emily Dickinson)

The film ended.
Stubbornly, we clung to our seats
As the credits raced into finality.
Mutely, we passed into the night
Still shackled by the strands
Of an interior world peeled open,
Laid bare, withheld from judgment after all.

Those souls who question the unknown,
Who doubt the unseen, yet grasp elusive faith,
Those missing the protective layer of deceit,
Burrowed deeply in the family fold,
Enveloped in the walls of home,
Impose a standard impossible to meet,
On both themselves and loved ones close at hand.

The flowers brought in from the outside world,
Artfully arranged to exhibit brilliant bloom,
Last but hours, then curl and wither, dropping their façade.
The teasing breeze fills the upstairs curtain
Bringing momentary balm to a raging mind
Exhausted from attempts to stem the ravages of time,
Exhausted from willing weak minds to avoid the brink.

The audience well knows the lesson laid starkly at its feet,
Grants that even genius cannot hold nature to the fire.
Yet hope abounds for a more reasonable world,
For the alternative, despair, holds us indoors forever,
Robs us of the flower growing on its stem
Or the child reaching for the moon.

Alex Edwards-Bourdrez

The Potbelly Stove

What is it about the heat
from the potbelly coal stove,
invoked by the preacher of gratitude,
that cracked our impassive countenance
to life in gentle, knowing smiles—
perhaps a memory unearthed?

Back then her walls, frail with poverty,
ushered the cold right into her veins,
numbed, she said, to the indignity of it;
a threat to the spirit rebuffed.

We settled into the invocation,
a globe of warmth to awaken
our child's heart, a retrieval
of our birthright spirit gone dormant,
a wordless embrace of what we had,
the silent music of the heat of love.

Bonnie Ellman

I looked at old photos, ornately wrapped in flowered albums,
I stretched my feet out comfortably, as the fall rain danced on the skylight,
and our pictures, like treasures, lay on the multicolored marble coffee table,
where there were once cup rings from recent visitors.
I played on the swings and my best friend would dare me to slide down
the pole,
I was scared at first, but I did, I used to be scared of everything
I used to cry because I wanted to die. Now I cry because I never want to die.

Melissa E. Filippelli

envious onlooker

i was envious of the moon tonight

all alone
in a pale blue
sun setting
orange, yellow, green
sky
not even a cloud
dared to take away from its beauty
by being near it
alone
high
sparkling
and watching
keeping its distance
unreachable by most
aware of its beauty
aware of its place in the world
aware of its purpose

i was envious of the moon tonight

Adam D. Fisher

Red Pepper

Pick up just one.
Feel the smooth
undulating red surface,
so smooth it seems polished.
See the green stem
in the middle of its wavy crown.
Take a sharp knife,
cut around the stem
to reveal
seeds clinging
to its placenta.
Cut in half lengthwise
and then into strips.
Notice how the red
goes nearly through
the quarter inch flesh.
Notice too how the inside
looks like a fine-stretched out-web—
passages for juice and flavor.
Finally, savor.

Denise Fisher

Caffeination Inspiration

(a rhyming rant in octameter)

A coffee cup, completely done;
bids me to seek another one.
The kitchen, two flights down, is far...
my inspiration is bizarre.

This drink needs it's 'accoutrements',
to make it's taste exubérante
A little sugar, maybe cream-
decide I must, my pallet's dream.

Some vanilla on Saturdays,
and some cinnamon on Sunday;
on special days some sweet whipped cream-
with Jameson's- (know what I mean?)

My caffeination choices sway
depending on my whims that day.
Realignment when disjointed...
redirection when miss- pointed.

Unless I'm suddenly inclined,
to take some tea of any kind;
So many flavors fill my drawer-
more choices now, need I say more?

How best to say what needs be said?
This notion rattles round my head.
Wayward words which vex and vary
seem obnoxious and contrary.

While wondering what path to take-
Coffee? Or Tea? (so much at stake…)
How many syllables will fill
a line whose weight is overkill?

I climb the steps back to my loft,
while contemplating words, as oft,
and in complexities I find
no answer to the questions rhyme.

What rhymes with orange pekoe tea?
What sweetener prompts most levity?
Sweet honeyed words cling to my tongue…
are some words old, are others-young…?

Wild winds are wailing at my door
to tempt the Spring sun I adore
inspirations wane and wander
tearing focus all asunder.

Branches beat a crooked rhythm
on the roof, and walls within them,
whooshing winds and the creaking walls
in counterpoint to meters calls.

I sip and know I'm happy here
I think and dream and then it's clear
the questions I must ask to learn
the ache I feel for what I yearn.

The answers seem more questions now
no balancing of 'why' or 'how'…
A pen is moved by many things,
and caffeine inspiration springs.

M. Frances Garcia

Disappointment

She laps at my soul
with insatiable thirst;
nothing can quench
the pain of what
might have been,
with patience and
kindness,
better understood
and accepted.
Rejected, plagued
by blindness, the
sins of another
mingle with my own
awareness of imperfection;
salt water is applied
to bloated tongue
as if to a jellyfish sting
yet brings little relief.
How might I escort change
to those closed to
introspection,
who spray the
mist of deception
in my rear view mirror,
who ignite the spark
too close to the gas pump
and dump simple acts

of charity into
the metal woven wastebasket?
There is nothing now
but patience. It's better to
walk away with small granules
of sand in my shoes than
to continue to excavate this
campaign of madness;
the drills are too close
to my sadness and their
vibrations shake my
tranquility. The black eel
in tall grass surrounds me.
Now I let go and
feel once more
what it means to live
so closely to
the shore. The tides
rise and fall;
castles dissolve
with waves of foam,
and seaweed clings
to my moist skin.
When I put
the seashell of life
to my
ear there is
no clear sound but
the silent roar
of my disappointment:
I quietly apply the ointment
of faith like tinted sunscreen
making sure to reach all

crevices in my neck, making sure that
all of the lotion is appropriately
distributed to arms, long legs;
knowing inside that
there is nowhere else to hide,
knowing that only this method
of self acceptance will block
ultraviolet rays, protect
against regret today.

George S. George

Eyelids

I entered the world with eyes shut, crying.
A nurse's gentle slap unglued my startled eyelids,
And the earth's light poured in.

In wonder I struggled to keep the lids open,
But soon learned that rest dwelled in
the sanctuary of closed lid darkness.

Through the years the lids would close,
Millions of times:
Savoring my love's early morning kiss,
Dipping into sleep's inexhaustible well of dreams,
Laughing at life's follies with mouth wide open,
Touched by music's poignant beauty
And memory's deep longing,
Breathing in of sweet fragrance,
Or shielding the eyes from smoke and dust
And the heart from images of pain and horror.

What a gift, this simple act of lid blink, lid open and shut,
And when the light has no live brain to tease,
A loved one, or a stranger, will gently shut the lids,
One final time.

Gina Giannetti

Petals and Thorns

You are
a creature of promise
blooming

Always striving for the sun
stretching towards the light
desperate for its warmth

But you grow in darkness
it consumes you
you bow and wilt
and it breaks my heart

I try to water you
to nurture you
but your roots are firmly planted
and I cannot move you
It is not for me to do so
Yet you demand it of me

Your pain took root in me
and I could bear it no longer
I had to step away

I cannot bear to be so close
to such deep sorrow

I miss your petals, dear one
but not your thorns

Tina Lee Gibbons

Mount Alumnus

We sat
perched on the cold concrete steps,
behind us stood our cloistered asylum,
in front, the waters of the Styx flowed swiftly
by us.
We laughed at life,
indifferent to what it would bring,
worrying not about the future,
nor the past.
but caring only for the moment…
We were indestructible.
Immortal and callow.
Our benefactors provided us
with the nectar of the gods.
We dined on the dreams of mortals
while the fountain of youth ran dry.
So very young,
so naïve,
so sanctimonious.
Little did we know
that it was our very lives
streaming by us.
If we had only known,
would we have tried
to dam up the river
to keep the life we knew then.
Would we have clung to each other

as unripe grapes cling to the vine?
Would we have kept the people in our lives
and not let go of the friendships we had forged
or
were we nothing more than
acquaintances,
sharing a moment in time,
that would only be remembered
when a shooting star
falls from the sky?
Where is everyone,
the mighty and the foolish?
Our Zeus's and our Diana's?
Our Pandora's and our Don Quixote's?
We came down from the mountain
to mingle with time
and lost our immortality.
We opened our boxes
and let our dreams escape.
We have chased and fought all
our windmills,
and now throughout it all
someday we'll be together again
at the top of the mountain.

D. Dolson Gregory

Lawrence Ferlinghetti in Three Short Acts

There's a chemistry that comes with age to stain the soul a sepia
and temper down the rage of old a photograph unwrinkled
where stubborn veins and vanity shape the cane unbended
become the tangled web we wove as weavers in the blended grove
Sorry and regretful for a memory that isn't yours
tours the vacant lot of land between the planned and banded
A staple in the canvas torn
A turn before the painted
Stretched against the tattooed skin
A lamp or soap remembered

And you're the one who raised a fist to mimic your biology
unable to do anything that rests outside of energy
but think about what you believe while weaponed in goodbye
invested in the right to breathe through interstitial lung disease
Or sing a song that marches on
the counterfeited window trim
A dusted star a scar and scorn
where someone else's skin is born
and chained against the law
before a mannequin uncoupled from the engine

Role the boulder down the hill and tell them about Sisyphus
How nothing ever broke the will of reaching for the precipice
Forget about the punishment shackled to the ankle
Inflicted on in innocence and tackled to the carrion
Of seeds to grow a tome unsown on lithographs and felting

You is the banker of the stone promoter of the fledgling
The broker of the tone in Sepia and sorrow
The windswept sand
The empty hand
The Corot of tomorrow

Aaron Griffin

Internet Obituary

Here lies the internet.
I thought internet was a pretty cool guy.
Eh linkd computers and didn't afraid of anything.
He died just like he lived,
Bound and wrapped so tightly, and so fully delietized.
He had fun once, it was awful.
And he taught me how is babby formed.
He was my best friend or brother, absolutely right now for sure.
Press (F) For Respects
Rest in peace in your glass coffin.

Marie Griffin

Approaching Afterlife

Often the decline begins
after the most climatic moment
as spring suicides
straight into fall.

For years you have walked
over your husband's bones
waiting for something to grow again.
Though magnolias still
explode along the fence
no one works the garden
at your old house anymore.

The crab apple where
the children played old black spider,
now pierces a bruised sky--
a reminder of how thorns
tangled in honeysuckles
will define a living pain
when pierced into skin.

Now the lawn is bare of children
from dawn to twilight.
Your children have left you
at the nursing home. You
refuse to take pink pills.
You gaze out the window

at the constellations
and believe even they have
lost faith in each other.

One day after you have
searched long enough
on those pink purplish evenings,
you will return to the pond where you kissed
underneath smirking stars
long retired after their last light.

Daryel Groom

I Teach The Kids That...

"To all of my students who have taught me that love is the greatest lesson in who you are and what you become."

I teach the kids that are the class clowns, misfits, loners, and criminals.
I teach the kids that maybe used to be in your class but now they are behind steel cages,
locks, and shackles.

I teach the kids that talk back and never talk at all.
I teach the kids who know more than me.
I teach the kids who got caught by the streets, got taught by the streets.

I teach the kids who have never learned to imagine,
because they only dreamed to survive

I teach the kids who are restless, relentless, and reckless
with a purpose.

I teach the kids you say refuse to learn, but I watch them grow and flourish
past all your honor students.

I teach the kids who have beaten all the odds because they are still alive
at 17.

I teach the kids who know four walls, institutions, and roll call.

I teach the kids who may not have heard, do your best! you will succeed!

71

I teach the kids who have been criminals but can be master entrepreneurs.
I teach the kids who have an edge, who have never been given an edge.

I teach the kids who have lived more life than most adults I know by 16.
I teach the kids who were never pristine, snow-white, or clean.
I teach the kids who learned to be mean before they could speak who learned to
be tough before they could scream.

I teach the kids whose reality is a common day nightmare.
I teach the kids whose dreams were never in reach.
I teach the kids with blank stares and orange jumpsuits.

I teach the kids with revelations and retributions to be fulfilled.
I teach the kids with gun smoke dreams and Al Capone ideologies.
I teach the kids who know more than my books and can read my mind before I speak.

I teach the kids who always wanted a chance to change but ended up here.
I teach the kids who are screaming with no sound.
I teach the kids no- else wants to.

I teach the kids who they say 1 in a million could make it out.
I teach each of these kids like they are 1 in a million.
I teach these kids because when they shine it is worth its weight in gold.

Maureen Hadzick - Spisak

Pruning the Family Tree

Research was difficult
Long hours searching archaic scripts
Hunched over tiny microfilm strips
I pat myself on the back
With each new find
I dig, prod and sniff
Like a bloodhound hot on the trail
Deeds and documents prove all is true
But now what do I do?
I see severed branches on the ground
Twigs wilted by strangled anger
But new growth is sprouting
From the strength of those roots
Nourished by lives, loves and secrets
All buried now
Do I prune this family tree
Or let the branches simply be?

Geneva Hagar

Musing of a Captain on a Sinking Ship

It is the sea---
        the sea
that born us
        the sea
that draws us to its domain
Set sail and
        the sea
will determine the outcome
Disturb tranquility
        the sea
will wake with a lion's roar
            Taken as a lover
        the sea
will surely betray
In response to our foibles
        the sea
will guffaw between waves
It holds secrets
        the sea
Knows locations of lost items
Places bets on my survival

Nick Hale

What a Doge!

fire alarms go off
in his head It's a 10
alarm on the horizon

eyes long as fish poles
tongue like red carpet
rolled out for the

who are you wearing
tonight klaxons add to
the choir of old car-horns

awoogaing smoke trails
to heaven above
limerence-mute

who could ever notice
the hint of
a suggestion

of dollar signs
forming in the corners
of her eyes

ready to make it rain

Sylvia Harnick

Waiting

I thrust my body
into the new spring air
eyes absorbing colors fair
purple crocuses push
the earth aside
lusting for the warmth
which the sun
leaves behind

dust teases new grasses
into silvery blades
dancing like young lasses
in a maypole parade

salt air coming on
wings of sharp breezes
I climb the hill
stopping to smell
the sea

Robert L. Harrison

The Alarm

The store alarm
went off at the exit
and he froze
not knowing
what it was all about.
The clerk asked him
to show his receipts
and if he was carrying
anything he never paid for.
After a quick check
there was nothing
hidden,
nothing stolen
and nothing not paid for.
Afterwards he thought
he must have felt guilty
about something
he forgot to buy.

George Held

New Era

A woman was reading from a new epic
About a shape-shifter born
Into a world without predator
Or even gender, its life a trick

Of the poet's eccentric
Vision. She hailed from Normal,
IL, and had survived tornado
Damage so catastrophic

That it left her allergic
To violence in any form
And so she invented warm
Creatures for her lyrical

Sci-fi and based it on the ecologic
Peril with which mankind had worn
Down Gaia-earth, the writer's scorn
Underscoring this fraught topic.

The audience were her peers,
Mid-fifties women stunned
By their crowns of graying hair, undone
By crows' feet 'tween eye and ear,

The shutdown of menopause.
The only man there was me,
And the women looked through me
Or, in surprise, dropped their jaws.

O brave new world, with such
A strange bearded creature in it –
Ignore it and maybe it won't sit
Long so insolently with us.

But I felt far from insolent,
Just alien in their midst,
Though curious about the gist
Of their pallid presence.

And at the end, after the cub
Leaves his mother, the applause
Leavening the room, away I slunk
Without delay, without pause

To have my book inscribed
By the sainted author, grateful
To leave intact, not ingested,
Like the Fisher King, in a ritual

Initiated by the sisterhood who'd
Gathered to welcome there
The epical shape-shifted child
Into a new era.

Diane Hill

Infinious

Even though thy beauty
outshines the brightest
star in the universe,
t'was thy gentle spirit
that captured my heart.
Thy soul is the other half
of my own.
Our love is a gift and a bond
that even death cannot break.
As dawn streaks
across the black night sky,
and I softly take my leave,
Remember, my dearest,
someday our eyes will meet,
our souls will reunite,
and we will be together again.

Arnold Hollander

We Come From Sundry Places

We come from sundry places
And have different views.
Our perspectives notwithstanding
We still have time to choose.

The moments of surrender
To feelings of ennui
Remain until we remember
Our life in days gone by.

And it's to those days that we retreat,
When all we see or hear is gloom
From a virus destroying our way of life
Leaving millions to face doom.

But it's in our own best interests,
To follow protocol:
Wearing masks, washing hands,
Keeping distance, a safeguard for us all.

The vaccines will arrive soon,
Millions of doses, or so I'm told.
Perhaps that is the answer
For those of us who have grown old.

Kevin Holmes

One letter

One number
Never wins
Pick a number
Find a letter
All hanging in balances unseen
Picked in dreams a dream
Or so it seems
To riddle to ridicule
I'll bet I bet one sure chance
Defined maybe pushed forward
Intuited more
I'll bet I bet on the score
A scene a scheme within a dream
Solid as laughter
I win

Idorenyin

Time Stamp

Since you left
I see dates differently
Calculated silently
By how little time
I had left with you
Calculated instantly
By how much time
I've been without you
Since you've been gone
I've had to act strong
But there is so much pain
Without any gain
Within my presence
Dealing with your absence

Maria Iliou

Angels Embrace

Connecting energies
Within your power
Powering my faith
In your palms

Whisper voice
Word of wisdom
Grasping trust

In a corner of
My mind, relaxes
Tranquil feelings
Sweeping through
My body flows naturally
In awe

Focusing on
Intensity within
Depth of lights
Appearing through
The window
Artistry design
Rejoicing view

Repetitively occurs

Luminosity shades, purple
Ebullience lights
Recurrently

In my vision
My eyes see
Angelic faces
Connecting souls
Reciting stories

The Angels
Camouflage
Surround you
Enveloping hug
Within light
Eternal love

Benevolent smile

Heavenly hug
Unveiling Angels
Sensing divine
Within innocence

Receiving energy
Absorbing higher sources
Standing grounded

Evie Ivy

Stilled Beauty
(or, The Resort 79 A.D.)

In Pompeii there are undone clay
vases, left the moment frightened workers
realized they were facing some coming doom.
Vases, under layers of ash and pumice
where Vesuvius closed life's day.
Vases for food and water left when potters

saw a giant pillar of black smoke spread
from Mt. Vesuvius into the infinite.
Life left unfinished. Words left in the air.
Uncooked and uneaten food. Hands suddenly
unclasped and clasped. What made a difference
suddenly does not matter . . . fear, terror

materialized in paths, and in the air.
Small and large feet scurried to the . . . where . . .
where . . . where . . . nowhere. . .
Remember . . . in the morning birds were not
singing. . .. No doors opened for relief.
No, "come to me" here or in Herculaneum.

Death came fast and slow, slow and fast
by a devastation, when nature and time wave
their fingers together, to say, "No more."

Jay Jii

Blessed Ventilation

Here

I gaze at an inspired sky
Clouds of satin, gossamer breezes
Smoke tango on a dance floor of firmament blue
Tendrils rise as marionettes on kite strings
To greet the open arms
Of memory

This thought
Keeps every fallen leaf
From the briar
Subdues the gravity
Within the situation
Narrows the discrepancy
Of satisfaction
Between a blown kiss

And *contact*

Give me
Your wayward zephyr
Symphonies of spring corollas
Come to fruition

In the wake
Of a swaying baton

I'll take your pocket
Of fresh air

And breathe it in

Edward John

In the Roots of Trees

Hurricanes form
In the roots of trees
Octopus mother
In herself believes
Huddles her brood
Against boiling seas
Hurricanes form
In the roots of trees
Corrugated hopes
Lift off like leaves
From blue roof tops
With spiraling ease
Dance above
For all to see
When hurricanes form
In the roots of trees

Ryan Jones

Center Of The Pentacle

Here I stand, high above the forgotten
The last seat of power
Central to fallen Atlantis
And the altars of civilization
Cast down through lack of sight
Obscuring savagery's divide
It was destiny that outpaced nature
Yet fate brought these waters
Lessons came too late to be learned
But such power will not be subverted

With the past which so few find beneath me
With the light above me
With the undiscovered in me
I stand here, in an unseen pentagon
Its planes ethereal
The undetectable confines
Through which the five intense views are focused
From afar, but not wide
Down paths ever tapering out
Cast in the five specific directions

I look to the south-west, and find balance
Where destiny and fate
Take different paths to the same result
The savagery within

By the course of nature's limits
Evades harmful change and struggle
With this sight I know volatility
With this sight I know strength
With this sight I know transition
The primal and unspoiled still prevail here

I look to the north-west, and witness loss
Where destiny and fate
Intertwine to consume all things
Nothing stands in the wake of desire's path
All is burnt and broken
Hunger's flames burn eternally
With this sight I know perpetuation
With this sight I know want
With this sight I know recklessness
The ashes of depletion reside here

I look to the north-east, and see change
Where destiny and fate
Go the way the other avoids
Where everything is exhausted
All efforts must produce
Recovery is reduction
With this sight I know consideration
With this sight I know need
With this sight I know regression
Reflection and regeneration rise here

I look to the south-east, and observe strife
Where destiny and fate
Are entrenched in direct conflict
Rampant exploitation and repression

Carve out the course of destruction
Forging nature's foothold
With this sight I know origination
With this sight I know life
With this sight I know mastery
The beginning and end fluctuate here

I look to the south, and greet ages past
Where destiny and fate
Collide to preserve what has been
Where the harsh veil of nothingness holds fast
To host disinterest
But change is inevitable
With this sight I know disestablishment
With this sight I know limits
With this sight I know wholesomeness
The preserved and vulnerable hide here

From this height of power and its five arms
I know all connections
A perfect circle links each point
Granting the mind complete circumspection
Extrapolating all
To divine each point's influence
That I may know how they are overlaid
And find each occurrence
To direct destiny and fate
Within the center of the pentacle

Amie Kachinoski

The Ugly Duckling

To cultivate oneself
To create one's abilities
Or create disillusion
To improve or be improved upon
I would rather be the vision
Than the shadow of doubt
Cast on raw ability
 Would rather shape natural beauty
 Than point out its flaws
 Prematurely
 Why criticize the ugly duckling
 Whose future is already destined.

Rorie Kelly

On Roads, Regrets and Legos

Regret is driving backwards on the shoulder
Of the highway to get back to the exit you missed
Only to realize
(Everyone staring at you in the rush hour traffic)
The one you actually wanted was the next one coming up
And now you'll never get there in time
Now you have to try to merge back in
Pleading with your hands
Imagining them smirking at you inside the other cars
It makes you just want to get off the highway altogether and take the long way
home.

Try to imagine for me, love,
A future where every next exit can be the right one
Where detours teach you the map a bit better
So when you finally near your destination
You know exactly where to turn and how to take a shortcut
Imagine this truth: that even if you run out of gas, someone is there for you.
Or this one: that no one else on this road knows where the hell they're going
either
The smirking ones the most lost of all.
Try to imagine that instead of scrambling to follow old directions
You make your own as you go
They can even include stopping at waffle house
Snapping a picture of a highway hawk circling

Taking a long nap at a family roadside inn
Try to imagine a life that you arrange to your liking
Rather than frantically trying to assemble a halfassed lego factory version
Of a dream you think has passed you by

Reimagine the dream only now you're the age you are now
Now, it starts where you live right now
Notice all the choices you are making
Do you want to live in a Lego castle
The prince of nothing in particular
Or do you want to begin proper work on your empire?
For sure you lack instructions
No built in moat
No plastic dragons
But maybe just maybe
You can build something new and magnificent
and this exit is the place to start.

Daniel Basil Kerr

The Philosophy of Uncle Fred

While I majored in business at Southampton College,
I minored in Philosophy.
Socrates said the unexamined life is not worth living,
Plato described thinking as the talking of the soul with itself,
and Descartes said I think, therefore I am.
Kierkegaard spoke of the Leap of Faith,
While Thurber said it was better to know some of the questions than all of the
answers.
Long before my undergraduate classes at Southampton,
I was introduced to the philosophy of my Uncle Fred,
who lived with my family many years in Asharoken.
He was from the Yogi Berra school of philosophy
where Yogi opined,
"You can see a lot by just looking."
Fred's philosophy of life had its roots in tragedy:
the death of both his parents,
the Japanese attack on Pearl Harbor,
the great Thanksgiving Eve train wreck on the Long Island Railroad,
the death of his dog Chubby,
and the theft of his car;
I think the last two were the most pivotal.
He kept clippings of Chubby's fur in an envelope,
and told me they ought to bring back the death penalty for stealing someone's
car:
"They hung horse thief's years ago,
I should be able to kick that guy who stole my car to death."

In between watching Saturday night wrestling on TV, (where have you gone
Bruno
Samartino?)
taking me and my four brothers to Ranger games at Madison Square Garden,

and baseball games at Yankee stadium,
Fred would ask us philosophical questions.
"What would you rather do;
die of the heat or the cold?"
"Would you rather go through life,
as a dog or as a man?"
"A dog doesn't have to get up in the morning, shave or go to work,
but you don't live long."
Fred seemed very wise when I was a kid,
but began to appear somewhat strange as I grew older.
"Don't stand too near the subway on the platform;
what would I say to your mother if I had to bring your body home in a plastic
bag?"
The post cards he would send,
from a large crematorium in upstate New York;
all the clippings he saved from the newspapers,
of fatal car crashes and other horrible accidents,
suggested a strange state of being.
The chain around his brake pedal and gas pedals,
and the padlocked cane attaching the steering wheel to the brake pedal,
as he put his new car to bed on our wooded acre of land in bucolic Asharoken,
suggested he never fully recovered from the theft of old car.
At his funeral,
My Mom said,
"I never knew if I had two husbands,
Or nine children;"
8 of her own,
and Uncle Fred.

As I placed clippings of Chubby's fur,
a New York Ranger's puck,

and a Yankees baseball in his coffin,
I recognized I was burying,
A beloved uncle,
My oldest brother,
and my first philosophy professor.

Laura Kolitsopoulos

A Moment in Time

Did you ever look or maybe peek with a squint in your eye
Did you ever chuckle at the thought and visualize the very reason why.
Did you ever fantasize something so preposterous
As you were staring at the ocean and heard it sing so sonorous.
Have you ever just wanted to be everything and more
And just laugh and sing and dance on the floor.
Did you ever just settle and look straight up to the sky
And did you ever just talk to yourself and ask questions, and reasons why
Did you ever adore the sun that shines and glistens right down into your face
And did you ever think of the things that would make you happy if you were
in a different place.
Did you ever think why do we live to follow the rules
Would it be so terrible if we acted like fools.
Just for a moment or just for a day
Just to act out how you feel
Without anyone staring in dismay.
Have you ever thought you lived a lie
Just because it was easy to get by
Did you ever wish you can start again
And never answer to where or when.
Are we a species of show and tell
And we have to decide either heaven or hell.
Are we who we are because it's right or wrong, and succeeding means going
strong.
So will you wake up tomorrow and subconsciously think you will win
Or will you just peak through the blinds
And stare straight at the sun

As her rays gallantly
Project a glamourous smile that forfills your endorphins.
Can you step aside and close your eyes and visualize who You are
Can you open your eyes and visualize
And say hey that's "me" by far .

Carissa Kopf

A Preschool Teacher Must Know

Up at six
The sun is still sleeping
Shower, pack the daily projects
Fill the coffee mug then out the door
Curricula rolling around on your mind
Punch in at eight
Classroom chairs pushed in
Name cards placed on the table
Paper and pencil neatly set
Storybooks waiting
Paint containers filled beside the easel
Letters, numbers, colors, and shapes
Already to be learned
The hustle and bustle is about to start

Right before the door opens
A preschool teacher must know
It's not tying laces
Wiping tears
Or changing soiled clothes
That teaches

It's that hug you give
When a family member is missed

Caring

Understanding a scraped knee from a fall
That you can still walk

Encouragement

A quarrel between two friends turns into a conversation
About friendship and sharing

Communicating

Giving the right tools
To be a artists, writers, dancers

Creativity

You set goals
Guide them to it

Achievement

It's the little things you do
To help shape futures

But just one thing
Please don't ever forget

There is no job more important than yours
You are a precious treasure
To every student that steps into your classroom

Michael Krasowitz

Overlord

This is the year of the lord 2459
This is my last posting
This is the day, the moment
The overlord ceased

It is said the overlord was created by us
Some 300 years ago
We made her to save ourselves
From ourselves

We made her from wires and metal
A daisy chain of dreams
Meant to synthesize all that was good
In a dying species

For we knew we could not do it alone
We cannibalized our culture and enslaved our brothers
In the name of progress
We could not govern our worst impulses

Imagine a place free of greed
Where no one owned
Where there were no borders
Where there was no want

That is the land of the overlord
Where we have thrived for so long

All was provided
We were content

The air is clear
Of the malevolence of the pleasure seekers
Those that chose to dominate
Were chastised and banished until reconciliation

Each year would be the great revival
A celebration and reminder of the past
Where the overlord would present herself
As a common woman amongst the people

I speak to you
People of the 21st century
As you contemplate the destruction
You are about to face

And it will be terrible
I know at least that much
As the overlord has protected us
From the relentless memories she holds in her databases

I am here to speak to those of you who will rebuild
And bring about the consciousness which will save you
Hold fast to the dream
I am proof and I have a question.

Why is the overlord leaving?
We are afraid we will become you again
The miserable and conceited
The hateful and violent

What did you program in her?
That would make her go away
Leave us to an uncertain future
Did you anticipate something we cannot see?

The overlord will cease to exist
The sun rises on a new day
I fear for the future
I fear the past in every fiber of my soul.

Mindy Kronenberg

By Design

If the page is a room, walk its lengths and corners,
Count the steps and turns and imagine how
To furnish with words,
Softening the corners with pillows
That surprise the eye, giving edge
To the seamless expanse as with
Occasional tables tumbled like dice.
Should there be a cone of light
Or pool of dark between stanzas?
Would it help to have a stairway
Twist and carry the reader
Down a flight to a floor
Carpeted with a river?
Let's create weather from *whether*,
Corridors of conundrums and answers
Summoned in enjambments,
And between the lines of closing doors
Echoing the hallways,
A window seeks a vista
In a bright place decanted from memory

Joan Kuchner

Vortex

I caught the glint in your eyes
as you rounded the corner.
Chase me!
And so it began.

Around the stairs,
down the hall,
through the family room,
into the living room,
past the door,
around the stairs.
Briefly, I stop.

Footsteps quiet.
Sidestep,
quick step.
then, back the other way.

I could catch you if not for the laughter.
I could catch you, but it would end the game.
Round and round we run
as the sprite I am chasing
swirls me into the fountain of youth.

Tara Lamberti

Out of nowhere lightning strikes:
an old forgotten song, snippets of strangers' conversations
something clicks and
 I am hand-touched by the Muse.
Divine phrases fill me up like air in a balloon
and I become conscious of why inspire means to breathe.
This craft is my life force.
In these magic moments
I am an extension of the Creator
fulfilling my soul's purpose with each word.
But inspiration is fleeting.
Once the masterpiece is written, there's another page to fill.
The harder I look for a spark, the more hallow I feel.
It's my creative curse.
I never know if lightning will strike again,
or if chasing it will be what kills me.

Billy Lamont

flattery 666 (emotional vampires)

words slit skin sub/tl/y
bleed/ing deep con.vic/tion
flat/ter.y's in.ten.tion

    emotional vampires
    suck your blood
    drain your soul
    feed off of your-

desire
your naked beauty
lies on the bed
wrapped in barbed wire

    you say,
    "don't tell me who i am
    & what i am-

feeling"
a spirit shrieks in the night
desparate
for healing

    "i know what it is like to be dead"
    i said
    long ago remembering

remembering
if a baby is not held it will die
& so i lie
holding myself & admiring you
until i whisper
"true agape love please ignite the-

fire"
on fire
with spiritual love & carnal animal lust
until skin is punctured by the rose's briar

the pure white sheets now run blood red
& i am left alone

needing
my soul lies bleeding

a distraction can lead to a deception can lead to destruction from emotional
vampires

Linda Leff

Joy Bird

Thin lines form slowly inside an evolving beech tree.
A charcoal sketch, gently laying down tracks,
Quietly outlining the vision of a small vibrant bird.

Did the tree know, while energizing its organic creation
That in the midst of nature's ring of years
a wedged imprint of a little bird would emerge?

A gift generously provided by nature,
hovering so vividly. A permanent miracle
perched in the heart of a wood tabletop.

Always a remarkable vision, dining with all
who dined, entrenched in family events,
bearing witness to household communal acts.

Did the little bird know that her soul
would spend eternity listening to life
spoken over her stationary wings?

Eleanor Lerman

True Hearts Marry

When I lived in the city
certain dark yellow hours were
driven straight to my poor, beloved street
Crates of rain were delivered with the mail
Old arguments camped out in the kitchen,
old grievances had my number—
but that was how I learned to write
That was the time when certain deviations
from the norm grew stronger
I let them. I wanted them to live

And still, great forces named in schoolbooks
put me to work in the Schoharie Valley,
where the creeks cackled to themselves
as they beat their fists against the houses,
churning out the breakfast biscuits
People threw pennies at the swans because
that is the currency in normal times:
granite, agate, cold intentions, though perhaps
not in the thoughts of women standing on
the hills above the valley, tall and industrious,
breathing in the chilly blocks of air

Oh love, how I have traveled!
Here and there, long and hard
Heartsick but industrious, I wore
oilskin in the winter, married because

I needed to be married, recovered from
the illnesses that are sold in the stores
of the Schoharie Valley and lied on
the journey that took me halfway
to oblivion. But remember: it is possible
that I also lied on the way back

So I think that I am old enough now
to have fulfilled my obligations to
the populace. Now I have a new message
for my friends who are gathering in the
poor, impoverished city, where the sun
arises with a new understanding: we thought
we were unhappy, but we were wrong

So we will get out the old banners,
strip ourselves naked and climb the
battlements of love. Watch the crows
fly towards the city with money in their beaks!
Women are baking the biscuits of resistance,
declaring that they are the brides of time
Thus am I able to declare that I have loved
my work with bread that is stronger than
any winter in a northern valley. *I love, I am,*
I do what I can to resist the deliveries of death
and poverty. I speak to women in my sleep

But remember: women never sleep
when they are in the city. True hearts
marry upon the battlements and only age
in the fleeting thoughts of swans

Iris Levin

Lost glasses

25 years ago we toasted
To that special beginning
To a new life together
To making it happen
To marriage
To I do
   I will
   I must
   I better
And now
To I can't
Those glasses filled with hope
Lost forever

Stephen Loomis

middle age

middle age should be your favorite pair of jeans
graced with the stains of a lifetime
frayed
threadbare
but soft
intimate as the knowing caress of well-worn cotton on old familiar skin
you can still squeeze into it
and it still hugs you back

Sheri Lynn

The Attic

Curled in a neat pile are
sketches of her arabesques
glinting among sun beam peeks
dust, webs do nothing
to taint his ballet of her
on each bronzed parchment
> *heart candle burn*
> *gold, indigo, orange*
> *pirouette meadow pink moon*

windswept windows vent
warm lilac perfumes and
songbird sonatas
evoking milieu from when
their arts, hearts, fused in
graphite and plies
> *heart candle burn*
> *gold, indigo, orange*
> *adagio aria glow*

letting his moist eyelids close
and fingers brush the pine floor
"Were you a mirage?"
paging through intrigue
in their once blooming loft
now his bare attic canopy
> *heart candle burn*
> *gold, indigo, orange*
> *brise water pane souvenir*

Cristian Martinez

Generosity

It disguises in many forms.
In selfishness, most close their wallets tight.
Having the misconception,
that giving money is the only way to demonstrate this act.
However, you can hold open a door,
to a stranger that can become valuable part of your world.
Letting someone have your time
Listening, with no judgment and being supportive.
You could volunteer however you choose.
Picking a cause that is passionate to you.
Helping those who need you to be there,
Assisting the forgotten, the voiceless in need of help.
Giving to a food pantry or donating your old clothes.
It must start somewhere.
Supporting a local business,
or a friend with a difficult disease.
Being generous with your time
Using it wisely,
It doesn't cost a dime.
If we all set out to be generous
With one act a day
A difference in so many lives
Can change the outcome of our days.

Kathleen Lynch McCarrey

Live to dream

While I wait, I straighten up
The dishes are done
The lights are on and door unlocked

Time passes and I tire so I go on up
I've locked the doors, and left a light on
He does not like the darkness

I fall asleep and he comes to me
He snuggles me and tucks me in
We laugh and talk and fall asleep

I wake and make the coffee
Only one cup, he does not like it
I make a list and wait, again he does not come
Somehow I shop, and when I put the things away
I see his cupboard is full, how can that be
I check, and they all expired a month ago
So I discard them and refill the shelf

I go through the motions of my day
It's late, so again, I lock the door
And leave a light on
I try to wait but sleep takes over
Then he comes to me and we make love
We laugh and hold on tight

Soon I realize this pattern and the expiration date
Always the same, it was his expiration date
So now I live to dream with him
Rather than dream to live with him
For it is only in my dreams he comes to me.

Rosemary McKinley

Harvest Moon

So big, and round, a burst of orange above us
It holds court in the sky
Commanding our attention
As we drive, the large, fiery ball seems closer to the horizon
Should it be?
It seems to move with us, ahead like the North Star
Guiding us east to our destination

John F. McMullen

A Poem As Picture

Some poets will
arrange the lines
of their poem in
a design to reflect
the poem's message

I am somewhat
in awe of the
additional time
spent by the poet
in choosing the
words and the
design necessary
to accomplish this
daunting task

Having said this
I don't like it

When I made a scathing
remark about such a poem
a poet friend responded
Some poets work at arrangement to shape the way the reader envisions the
meaning

Ok
I get that
BUT
In the words
attributed to
movie producer
Samuel Goldwyn
Include me out

I want poems
in plain English
that tell me what
the author feels on
a particular subject

I recognize that
many feel that it
is the responsibility
of the reader to
work at a poem
to understand the
nuances intended
by the poet

On occasion, I am
willing to do that
if the subject or
the poet have
interest to me
but I resolutely
draw the line
at deciphering
cartooning

Mollie McMullan

She Pecks

I know a girl who bakes but doesn't eat,
sleeps but doesn't dream
Often, I wonder if she wants to stop shivering,
turning the thermostat to 78 degrees to replicate the fire she's lost
She's a baby bird perched on a live wire

Gaunt cheeks are disguised with blush,
glazed eyes framed by thick eyelashes
Her spinal column breaks through thick cotton sweatshirts,
knees knock together even in sleep
If she was art she would be Poblenou's Kiss of Death

Self saboteur,
you have more power than you realize,
more control than you can begin to imagine
You're the only one with the reins

Gene McParland

It Was a Simple Thing

It was a simple thing.
Heck, it was only a smile
exchanged between two strangers;
a sunny easy-to-give smile;
no costs involved,
no deep hidden meanings.
Just one face
looking briefly into another's.

It was a form of recognition
of another's humanity.
But like the early morning light
spreading across a dark landscape
erasing the night,
the smile helped
make the day
worth living for another soul.

Just think - it was only a smile
that did all that!

Heather C. Meehan

Survival

Ridged blue mussels
stacked on the shoreline
each clasped shell
impenetrable.
We pace our quiet houses.
Tuck ourselves in.
You act as if
this isn't how it's always been.
Seagulls shriek, plucking mussels
from their ranks.
Rise on the winds,
perfectly positioned
to crack a dropped mollusk.
The gull survives on broken boundaries.
The mussels rely on solid horizons.
The sky's emptiness
blankets both evenly.

Lisa Meyer

Haven

Flawless, jagged beaches
Seagulls song
A fort now forgotten
Connecticut shore
Kindred New England lighthouse
Peaceful fisherman's pier
Weathered wooden playground
Modern skylines appear
Craggy, sandy cliffs and
Ancient morning mists
Play with pages of my youth
On resilient Long Island Sound

Lisa Mintz

Questionable Questions

Do you worry that you will miss the mark?
Do you fret that your dreams will be left in the dark?
Are you certain that things will slip away
In the damp, dark corners of the newborn day?
We all wonder the same, the questionable questions
The annoyances of our own imperfections
We sit by the wayside and ponder reflections
Uncertain unknowings that bring new directions
All of us feel the same tuggings of heart
The trick is to realize that life is like art
A constant unfolding of brand new creations
Our wonder and awe take us past trepidations
We meet in the middle to keep our life flowing
And in doing the work, we achieve joy & growing
So the next time you panic, or fret, or feel stress
Just remember it's something we all will address
Be gentle, be kind, fall in love with yourself
Your life is a book, live it off of the shelf!

Amanda Montoni

Tattooed Sleeve

your tattooed sleeve
somehow makes me believe
our souls were meant to intertwine
like the ink that lines
your skin
let me in
but please oh please
don't slip me from your memory
like a forgotten tattoo
that you, oh you
once gleamed and glanced
at with eyes that danced.

CR Montoya

Of Dogs and People

To paraphrase Henry Higgins,
why can't people be more like dogs?
Dogs do not judge
do not care about the breed(ing),
color or size of other dogs,
they regard all with the same inquisitiveness
and a sense of adventure.

Dogs' behavior is consistent;
a negative interaction
or ungracious greeting
doesn't change their demeanor.

They each possess an individual personality,
yet they still manage to accept others
whether two or four legged.
Dogs can discern sincerity and caring
from the opposite,
they respond enthusiastically to kindness,
are quickly bored by indifference.

While dogs desire our attention,
if we fail to respond, they move on
without a display of arrogance or anger.

Dogs learn quickly and willingly,
though they may require some training

they don't require college
or its attendant costs.

Dogs give their love and loyalty unconditionally.
They are the first to greet us when we arrive home.
Even if their objective is for a treat,
There's no complaining if none is offered.
Doesn't this devotion deserve recognition,
A reward, a back scratch, or just some undivided attention?

Dogs know how to have fun and know their limits;
They understand the value of the power nap.

While they have their disagreements,
They never hold a grudge
And carry on as if the event never occurred.

Dogs accept their circumstance
Without grousing or complaining.
They adapt and deal with change
With the wisdom of a scholar.

Dogs are unique,
With qualities - humans should emulate.
Imagine if all the people living in the world
Possessed the virtues of our canine friends,
How much better the world would be,
A better place to raise our dogs and families!

Imagine this world!
John Lennon did.

Sean Richard Morris

What is art?

Art should not draw attention to itself.

Art should stand in opposition to all things.

Art should make you aware of the room you're standing in, and everyone standing in it.

Art should blind you with thought to the point that when you get back to yourself you're embarrassed about how lost you got without taking a step.

If it doesn't do that, then it's not art.

Mary Sheila Morrissey

My Day

My day microwaves
bombarded
with many things sometimes
overheating me but leaving my
core still cold
My day agitates and spins
overloaded leaving me
lopsided and
inefficient
My day vacuums
pulling up and into
my head all kinds of debris
and discarded thoughts
My evening downloads and updates
images and words for
future reference
My night commutes sometimes in
heavy traffic but once in a while
takes a winding route thru
a meadow

Dianne Moritz

The Dunes at Wyandanch Beach

The dunes are mostly gone now.

Remember how we played fetch
with my dog and you took a piece
of driftwood, etched "I love you" in sand?

We made love up in the dunes, the sun
on your back, a fire through me, lust
sprinkling down like a warm sea mist.

Once I watched as you swam, sleek as
a dolphin, body-surfed with new friends.
I called out, but you didn't hear.

The dunes are mostly gone now....
washed away by time and tide.

Ian Murdock

I Saw

I saw a **Mountain**
It muscled to the sky
Majestic and strong
Its rugged flanks
Hoisting its frosty crown
To tear the jet stream

It did **not** bend to me

I saw a great **Ocean**
Unfathomable in depth
An expanse beyond a hundred horizons
So fearsome in its rage.
And so sublime in its calm
The cradle of life on Earth

Its tides did **not** alter for me

I saw the timeless **Sun**
Holding the planets in its embrace
The mighty center of a great celestial dance
It scorches the Sahara
Power to heat the globe
And make the full moon smile

It did **not** blink for me

I saw the **Milky Way**
Traverse Heaven's great arc
Introducing man to infinity
Our very meaning questioned
Channeling cosmic mystery
From the soul of God

It did **not** acknowledge me

Then

I saw you...

Ed Nardoza

9 A.M. Mass

At the margins of enforced sincerity
Strict, wimpled women
And men in important hats told us,
Lift up your hearts.
Shaken awake
A love of the explicable,
Dusk's summoning home,
A compendium of early ventures,
Skinned knees, difficult kisses,
Bouncing balls, buck-buck,
Bottle caps and freeze tag;
The girl across the nave,
The one who looked back at you,
Hair bobby-pinned with a patch of lace,
The sun an aspergil
Through stained glass.

Marsha M. Nelson

Death: The New Cancel Culture

"Each man's death diminishes me,
For I am involved in Mankind
Therefore, send not to know
For whom the bell tolls
It tolls for thee
                    ~John Donne

Shiva is doing a death dance at CERN's portal.
We keep the blood on the doorposts
of our hearts.

A plague on all your households.

Another layer of the veil is rent.
Evil the palpable arm with fingers-
reaching.
Pandora's box is open.

Ascending the shift-
New York has become the new Killing-Fields
as the poorest of its neighborhoods get decimated.
She suffers the sword of a faceless phantom.
His sickle wet with poison-
coronavirus.

Corona, Queens crowned sovereign
of the diseased.

Stacked bodies are seen outside
of hospitals and funeral homes
and the death toll is the highest
in the rise of the pandemic
on that side of the tracks.

George H Northrup

Subject to Change without Notice

It was drafty at home
when all the doors disappeared.
I didn't mind the missing steeples,
stop signs, Styrofoam, student loans,
war zones, end zones, calzones,
complete works of Fill-in-the-Blank,
several stages of grief.
Vanished: boons, banes, and bugaboos.
I hardly noticed when all the Bureau Chiefs
went out to lunch, never to return.
Soon there was not a monad or a syllogism
left anywhere on the planet,
no double takes, clam bakes, spring breaks
no B. S., no P. S., no T. S. Eliot,
no hollow men or ragged claws,
neither a bang nor a whimper
amid the plunging decrescendo
of favorite symphonies. I looked in vain
for fast balls, fast cars, fast food,
grandes dames, blame games, street names.
I would have asked the few remaining
carpenters for new doors, but by then
housing had imploded.

I didn't miss
paper money, papier mâché, pay per view,
pratfalls, pitfalls, windfalls, cat calls.

I knew only a few of all the people
once named Flynn and Gonzalez.
No dreadlocks, headlocks, wedlocks.
Where are they now—the secret handshakes
and gentlemen's agreements,
boycotts, tomboys, home boys, choir boys,
boy toys, game boys, killjoys?

Sparrows hopping in the snow disappeared,
then every type of winged and feathered aviator
that once had nested in the former trees.
Things stopped slipping through my fingers
once I lost my fingers.

Shock and dread began to spread like plague
until these, too, withdrew, along with ragtime,
tea time, half time, bedtime,
one or more Persons of the Trinity
(the exact number not disclosed),
and everything sweet except you—
then you.

The end of glaciers had been foretold,
but not the pale voids
where primary colors once gleamed,
not the faltering grip of gravity,
time's drastic tachycardia.
History vanished in a noisy gulp,
like a treasure-laden galleon
into the Devil's Triangle.

A billion stars winked shut
in this obscure galaxy
once proud of its epoch.

See, now, the infinite surplus of future events,
the inexhaustible spare change of kinetic energy
funnel down to the last drop of dew
poised to evaporate beneath a blighted sunrise.

Gloria O'Lander

Hello Mom, Hello Dad

Walk outside I head to the side yard.
I stop a moment to say hi to Dad.
We converse a moment or two.
Then to the backyard,
Where Mom is
We laugh as we share some memories.

You see, I have two gardens.
One is for Dad – the Buddha garden.
A circle of rocks, beach glass & plants. In the middle sits a Buddha.
My Dad was known as the Buddha.
He certainly had the patience and insights of one and that special smile.

Mom's garden has large rocks with several plants inside.
In the middle sits a tall lighthouse, handcrafted by Amish craftsmen.
Mom loved her lighthouses - they were all over her home.
I guess you could say she was the beacon of our family.

They are gone now, they have passed over.
But they are not forgotten.
Memories of them and their spirit lives on.
It's nice to visit them In quiet moments and share my day with them.
My gardens are a living memory of family.

Tom Oleszczuk

Five deer

Two, four deer,
no, five (!)
run
       across
                  the country road
no cars now, except mine

Only a young couple walking a mile up
oh, I see another pair
another mile away
coming in this direction
no sidewalk
minuscule bike path
no cars

Ah, a bicyclist vigorously pedaling
up the wooded hill
no cars,
few people

At the recycling center
a few cars and people
I see a friend
chat at six-feet

He tells of a neighbor
yesterday walking along

the wooded, curving
 road
 struck by a speeding sports car
and
 left
 in the dust
 the driver speeding away
One car
one person

Sherri London Pastolove

Summer Sonata

It was the low rattle of
old air conditioners that
lulled me to sleep
my little body tired
from hours of dodging waves
and digging sand –
a pink shovel and flowered pail
my prized possessions -
burying my brother
with determination until
his body was no longer visible
only neck and head
tilting upwards
grinning in the blazing heat
hours later
chocolate ice cream, rainbow sprinkles
my tummy filled with delight
then tepid water
under a trickling showerhead
my sun-kissed skin
lathered in Noxzema
a soft flowered nightgown
tucked in that lumpy bed
my bathed toes
still depositing
small grains of sand
into thin lines on the

scratchy motel sheets
my eyelids feeling heavy
slowly closing as
the neon lights
crept beyond the edges
of worn curtains
flashing
"welcome summer guests"

Marlene Patti

An ode to books

A book is not decoration
or used to fill a color scheme
or hold a glass on a table
or carry in your backpack
like an old snack,
a book is a mind
a book is a time
a book is a mood and place.

A book sets a tone
you cannot let it be wasted
or use it to fill a space.
A book has a pulse-
a beating and dreaming
heart that wrote it
as those words
were careful placed
for you to almost taste!

A book cannot be
chosen in haste
because a book
always chooses you
it calls out your name
when you need it most,
because like humans
books have meaning
and therefore a book
is *not* a damn decoration!

Mary C. M. Phillips

bird

a sullen tuesday morning
awoken by a bird
a sparrow there upon the sill
who spoke no single word

yet brought a sense of happiness
I can't fully describe
that simple joy of flight within
that's glad to be alive

so quick a visitation
grateful in just seeing
oh how i wish he'd build his nest
deep within my being

Kelly Powell

Master of the Custodial Arts
High School for the Performing Arts, Syosset, 2009

They leave love notes and lunch boxes
history lurks in her seams, bricked
into walls, bursts from gum
beneath her desks and from
the piles of the lost and found.

First in, last out with a mop—
its spongy, white strings
his instrument, glides across
the width of a hallway—
as a camera would pan its length,
medium shot to long shot

showing the hallway
in perspective. Diminishing
space of asbestos tile leads toward
a vanishing point of open, empty metal
doors lying across the horizon line.

Beckons the outside world and
the fighter of rubbish pirates. The keeper
of his mistress' secrets. He shines
her brightwork of lockers and runny,
tarnished faucets. Folds away layers

of chairs deep within her hold. Flightless,
nameless bird, proud of his flock
as they leave the nest. Others arrive
as new leaves fall—tides of yellow
and browns—merge with orange and reds.

They scatter and decorate a muddy,
forgiving earth. Performance ended
he closes the light, whistles
and shuts the door.

Sharon Renzulli

Harvest Moon Eve

The awning's canvas is a blowsy sail as I lie on my second-story deck in repose--taking in the hot Sun which smells like a warm baby on my skin.

Listening to the mighty Atlantic, a mere ½ mile away, I'm struck by the realization that
we are on the great Mother Ship coursing through the heavens.

The sails flap continually, moved by the soft, zephyr breeze of late, late summer.

For a second I wander off, wondering who's at the helm. No matter.
Be still and know...

Navigation points fixed. Steady as she goes as I check the compass rose.

You were the great storm of my life. We rode it out to the tumultuous end.
Within that storm was our great song that moved out over the world. (Rilke)

I spent my bereavement in dry dock, repairing the hull; stitching the canvas— living at times in the hold. But now, I'm seaworthy again and ride the swells with great anticipation.

Tonight's the night we can dance by the Harvest moon. Shadow and light so deeply etched in the evening—reaping till the dawn. The immense quiet opens into a deep-space silence and you can hear the smooth, seamless moving of the Earth—and sense the quiescent immensity of our universe.

The pre-dawn sky is satiated with stars and a quarter-moon is low in the Eastern sky.
There's an other-worldly stillness as I gaze at magnificent Orion and his trailing Sirius. The rapacious Taurus stalks the frightened Pleiades.

I float and bob into worlds so exquisitely sublime—all so beautiful—so water-weighty that it breaks into sadness—like so much flotsam.
The miracle of Life buoys me and I commence to construct a raft and ply with courage again.

Diana R. Richman

It's Up to You

Covered or caressed
Smothered or soothed
Provoked or protected
Reality is reflected by your mood.

Chosen or picked on
Fitting in or one of a kind
Provided privacy or ignored
Reality is created in your mind.

Unique or really weird
Accepted or out of favor
Gifted or diagnosed
Reality is inferred from your behavior.

Mystical or wise
Impulsive or true life force
Obsessive or conscientious
Surrender to reality is a life course…
of acknowledging

War and peace
Beauty and the beast
Pride and prejudice
Newborns and the deceased   .
Good health and disease
Poverty and success

Power and vulnerability
Giving up and doing your best.

What choices do you make?
It's not all good or bad
It's not all happy or sad
It's not all angry or glad.

It is all up to you
To transform from "or" to "and"
Accept life's daily paradoxes
Invite your being to expand.

Daily struggles present a challenge
Of ease and discomfort each day
So, welcome the unexpected
And trust your soul to find its way.

Allie Rieger

Here

Home is coffee made
at 1:00 a.m. so I get back okay,
since I was just falling asleep in your bed.
Nestled into the corner of you
where your neck meets your body -
the softest skin I've ever felt.
My head on your chest
listening to the sound of
living.
Better than any insect song sung on a summers night.
Any morning glory bird calls beckoning me out of bed.
And to think that just
six months ago, here,
my clothes were on a strangers floor

Martin Rocek

Sanderlings

the waves slide up the sand, nononono
the pipers pedal back above the froth
yesyesyesyes they chase it down and fro
and poke the swash and search and back and forth

like prospectors who pick but stake no claim
they pause or run or walk but never stand
and nonono again each wave the same
and new each time the foam sinks down the sand

Adele Seagraves Rodriguez

My Maine Coon kitten
emitted noxious odors.
Silent but deadly.

Coronavirus:
on tee vee and in the news
twenty four-seven.

My time was not mine
going through thirty-three days
of radiation.

Rita B. Rose

Pandemic Skateboarder

Covid on a skateboard rode by today
no face covering, no gloves
red T-shirt draped his shape
neon yellow shorts highlighted
his gray and black sneakers
he wore a grin as wide as a viral brim

As he skated past
I pointed to my mask
thinking his youth
offered invincibility
he chuckled—I warned—
This virus will force you to your knees
Covid on a board dismissed me
with a wave and rolled along

Silly boy, you cannot push off what
you do not see, death will be your last wish
you better bail—isolate—skate home
or this bug will *high jump* you
to heaven above!

Marc Rosen

Those days have come and gone

In days of faith and youth
In times where hope could prove
In ages when my innocence did reign

A hero, I would be
I would make history
A world improved would carry forth my fame

Those days are dead and gone
Those days are damned and lost
We dance along the vagaries of yore

The world turns on its ass
My hopes have been outclassed
I'd carry on, but it's been such a bore

I danced along this thread
And held up till the end
I followed it as far as it would go

And thus I must conclude
The real world did intrude
And so for now, I disregard my woe

It didn't matter then
It doesn't matter now
It never was more than a fevered dream

My dream was but a farce
For I'm naught but an arse
But for myself, it might have been achieved

A. A. Rubin

Snow Ghosts

and the snow falls like tiny ghosts,
translucent 'neath the pale moonlight—

crumbs fallen from the Reaper's hand
as he squeezes the life out of harvested souls

as the wind whips them around,
they coalesce—frantically—

disparate   parts

seeking for partners
with whom to form bodies,

but they end up mismatched and incomplete,
portmanteau, stitched together—

—mere shells. Empty and ephemeral—
rising in gothic gusts in the midnight chill.

you hear them howling in the storm.

you tell yourself it's the wind, but—
deep down, you know it's not

you pull your blanket over your head and hug your children tight.

as the soul flakes flutter,
frantically searching for living beings to haunt—
—not out of any need to complete unfinished business,
but out of a desperate desire to avoid the nothing that lies beyond—

Christopher Santiago

by dawn
and all that is unwritten
by love
and all that is unloved
I declare:
YOUR SOUL! I SAW IT!
gnarled in the wooden gods
on the hill obscured by street lamps
I saw it in heroic frenzy running down King Street
wake up congested brain breath
wake up dry and panic of dream
knife fights just to get home
don't let anybody know (about death)
you're just a pathetic amorphous
creature don't let the university find out
don't let the professors know
that brain breaths are of the world
a gnarled god on schizophrenic hill
and that the street lamps are cops
for animals whimpering in unborn day
the moon was a swollen belly
a pregnant ivory pearl of bone
plump corpuscle of wakefulness
that awareness that just won't quit
the grey adult suit that tears you
away from crepuscular womb
nestling

Robert Savino

If I Was God

If I was God
I would feed the multitudes,
my beard would be longer
to nest a civilization.

If I was God
disciples would walk along
the open road and read from my book.

If I was God
I would walk across Fire Island beaches
forgive the sinners.

If I was God
I would be the universe
the sea, sky, land, all uninterrupted space.

I would touch everything.
I would ignore nothing.
If I was God
I couldn't be me.

Joseph E. Scalia

A Broken Bar of Moonlight

A broken bar of moonlight
shattered silently
the window glass,
snaked along the hallway,
stole across
the hard wood floor
into the bedroom,
climbed the wall
to the mirror
where it shined
into closed eyes,
burrowed deeply
into sleep,
hardly disturbing
my dreams.

Thea Schiller

Oh. Oh Oh to the Ode of Ordinary

Breathe in, fill lungs, sun's a coming
Sweet conversations sans drama, lifting the palm of your right hand,
Glide it over your left arm; life is good.
Count on the customary
Establish a mountain, a misted movement in your mind
Close your eyes
Breathe in, expand lungs, sun's a coming
Barefoot, skip over to your closet
the place of satins, silks, linens and cotton
Choose wisely
Forget hiking gear, clunky boots, heavy woolen socks
No need, It's summer
And the mountain is in the misted movement of your mind
Select the flowing raspberry v neck sheath, just long enough to feel the fabric
on your shins
Drape a white chiffon scarf,
 Embroidery of tiny red birds will delight
Black patent leather sandals, thin strapped, can adorn your feet
Instep or Outstep
The misted mountain is in your mind
Place a natural-colored wide brimmed hat
On your head, gently,
Your curls near the ears will be free to roam
This new custom sets

Walking the path ascends to twilight
You are almost complete,
And if you're wondering about tomorrow,
favor yellow chiffon, or baby blue silk
 to greet the sun.

Sophia Schiralli

Insomnia

So sick as I lay in bed
alone with my thoughts
wish they were you instead
my pillow beside me
should be your chest
your arms should be close
so close, that i can hear you
breathe, your heartbeat
a melody if you were near me
i'd hold you so tight
the sheets wouldn't
even stand a chance

Karen Schulte

A Matter of Some Importance
(*from an old Kodak photograph*)

Whatever could I be saying
wagging my finger at another child

About a year or two older
or at least a foot taller

Both of us in profile
faces obscured by bonnets

Next to grandpa's store
down the hill from main street

Deep in discussion
with an urgency I have yet to outgrow

Or so it seems from a lifetime
of hits and misses

But at three or four years old
I can only guess

From the image of two children
one looking up, the other down

Engrossed in a deep matter
of solving some problem

In our warm clothes with parents
close by taking our pictures

With not much to worry about
except to wonder

If the next train to roll over the tracks
would be on time at 3 0'clock

And would the engineer wave to us
as it passed?

Christina Schlitt

Allegiance

Nation's flags unfurl as do leaves all over the world.
The leaves pledge no allegiance to country, leaders, society.
They heed only the call of the warmth of sunshine
Urging them to emerge anew each Springtime.
Nor do they respond to the cries of hateful nationalism
Thinly disguised as patriotism.
Mother Nature is their only leader whose wails are not heard
By all of mankind; her destroyers.
Humans forget that we, too are her children, as are the leaves
And all their plants and trees; all the creatures of lands and seas.
To Her should be our primary obligation
Not to a party of Democrat or Republican.
Wasteful consumerism that throws garbage in Her face.
Is our greatest sin of selfishness – our biggest disgrace.
Can she ever survive our desecration?
Most of her children, tens of thousands of species,
Brought to extinction – or its brink.
How is it that we've forgotten
To who we owe our obedience?
It is to Nature and Her Creator, we owe our allegiance.

Barbara Segal

shelter 18

a hawk floats
to a nearby branch

i walk five steps
look back…vanished!

along the harbor shore
two dozen crows

—that's a murder!—
fly southwest

tonight's full moon sends
silver through my window

pulsates
possibility

this morning a squat dark spider
scuttles across the kitchen sink

i catch and release her
without harm

[memory: hiking
in a state park forest—

a black bear
nearby through the trees

lumbers parallel to me
along the ridge]

close encounters can be
encounters too close

Jacqueline Shortell-McSweeney

Perspectives

-

Red sun pierces afternoon haze
and ocean reaches for white sand.
Senses tangle in metaphors of gender as
we unravel mystery, one in the other, on indigo sheet.
In solemn rite, you recite your poems to me,
the surf your chorus.

Bikinied girls on sultry blankets
wonder at these two so coupled in verse,
hidden in the shadow of the stripped umbrella.
As desire sketches an ancient seascape in pale strokes,
words embrace.

Ray Simmons

The Firefighter

They rested
a while near the
32nd floor
the stairway packed
with an unending stream
of people
some too
numb to speak,some
offered bottled water
A woman touched
his hand and said
"God bless you"
He knew it was
bad, maybe worse
than `93.
It was getting hotter.
His turnout gear hung
on him like
a wet heavy blanket
and that house fire smell
multiplied by a million
The Lt. came back,
said "Time to go,Gentlemen"
He stood up,
shifted his Scott Pak,
picked up the Haligan
& the axe.

He peered into
the smoky darkness
whispered
"You and Me, Lord"
and climbed straight
to his death
like a man.

Diane Simone-Lutz

Long Island Spring, 2020

The streets are silent save
chimes, sparrows, squirrels.
Starlings nest in the birdhouse,
clumsy darlings carry sticks that won't fit
through the doorway—the doorway
that isn't smeared with blood, as ours should be,
except that Dark Angel cares nothing for ritual and hymn.
This time, masks and gloves
and space between us is all we have to stave
the viral hive.

Cherry blossoms spill pink petals,
daffodils droop at our front stoop
where no one dares to pass--
lest we die alone
without goodbye
hands or prayer
the anointing, the robes
the sacred stone.
The morning light procession.

Leslie Simon

Her Garden

it's a faint whisper
she strains to hear,
trees speak of breezes
a harmony of soft rustling

everything listens

songbirds sing sweet refrains to the heart
they stop and say prayers
the joy in the symphony
embraces her soul

her garden porch is the secret
a tranquil space
private thoughts
a gift to her senses

the wind's breath
scatters seeds of fresh paint...

glossy greens
goldenrods of deep yellow
gracious gladiolus
glorious crimson geraniums
golden daylilies
grand scent of lavender perfume

all drift into her soul…a pastoral trance

simplicity of moments
swirl in her being
sustain her mind
assign peace within

Vijaya Singh

Sometimes

Sometimes I sit and I ponder and I think that maybe we can all be happy...
Sometimes I sit and I ponder and I think that maybe some of us aren't meant
to be happy...
Sometimes I sit and I ponder and I think that maybe I'm just going to have
fleeting moments
of happiness in a lifetime of sadness

Emily-Sue Sloan

If Only I Could Draw

I would release all the words
stored up in my language house
to be snagged by another poet or songwriter.
Please, have at them.

I'd much prefer to show than tell you,
but pictures turn to verse
before my clumsy hands
can guide them onto canvas.

So I am left with words —
nocturnal, feral. They paw
through sleep's deep layers,
clamor for attention, then
bunch up silent in a sunlit corner.

When I poke at them, they scamper off,
taunt me into a game of hide and seek.
Long after I've lost interest, they turn up
again with those sad eyes, looking
to be welcomed home.

Barbara Southard

Three Weeks Offline in Alaska

Fast-rushing streams
Digging out their chosen course
Bears picking through soap berries
Bones bleached white
Lying where the last stand occurred
Or where bitter wind took its claim.

There's an order here
A logic that can be followed
Counted on
Another language used
Visceral, kinetic
Intelligence of a different scale.

Toni-Cara Stellitano

Easter Morning (Forty)

Pacing in my apartment
the morning after Easter,
a phone call with my mother,
all I did was say I couldn't do the crowd,
"I cant do the crowd"
(I'm turning 40)
Fifteen pig headed, small minded, Italians
together in one house,
Their mark of good citizenship,
the stigmata on their hands,
and thorn crowns upon their heads,
"yes, come and eat at our banquet Child,
just so long as you have a ring on your finger,
and a baby inside"
All I did was say I couldn't do the crowd.
It isn't like I didn't want children,
images of pregnancy filled my journals for years,
My relationships with men never seemed to work out,
my career goals always did -
Who am I to argue fate?
Who am I to direct God?
Maybe if I had been nurtured rather than condemned,
that marriage in my 20s might have ended differently
and that fibroid in my womb,
might have been a grandchild for you instead.
Maybe then, I could have met that insatiable need of yours
to be loved,

had I given you the gift of lineage -
I. Will. Not. Give. You. The. Gift. Of. Lineage
Anger and Blame.
Overall, I feel happy, when I step outside
of EXPECTATION and CONVENTION
there is a FREDOM here
that no Mother can know,
A fluidity and an excitement,
a PRIVILEDGE even,
To live a life of my OWN.
I saw it clearly 2 years ago,
curled up in a ball on the floor of a Hari Krishna temple,
a chain tied to your clitoris, while mine MULTIPLIED
in intergalactic dimensional bliss,
sprouted butterfly wings
and flew away
"BUCKET!" *
Forgive my regression around such things,
its' just that I'm turning 40
and I don't understand how me saying
"I cant do the crowd, lets do coffee instead "
translates as "I don't love you."
Victim.
I called you that,
pacing in my kitchen the morning after Easter,
after you hung up on me,
and made your feelings my fault.
 "I am not responsible for your feelings, Mother,"
all I did was say that I could not do the crowd,
My ego felt too fragile,
my birthday felt too close,
and I might have shared that sooner,
BUT. YOU. WOULD. HAVE. TOLD. THE. CROWD,

Vulnerability is not sacred, and boundaries are not known,
forty years of blood in intimacy Mother,
and I cannot do your crowd.

*This refers to a hallucination that occurred during a plant medicine cere-
mony, where physical purging is part of a healing process, yelling and call-
ing for a "bucket" is what happens just prior to a purge

Ed Stever

Participation Is A Major Portion Of Your Grade

There's a god
I pray to every day,
and when nothing comes to pass
that I beseech of him/her,
I am never disappointed.
But just once,
I would like to taste
the residue of a miracle,
nothing phantasmagorical,
merely the flash and powder
of simple prestidigitation,
a life where suffering
is locked in a tabernacle,
the key lost,
on the altar of a god
who nobody
believes in.

Lennon Stravato

Nashville

Headin' down to Nashville
on the fumes of a desperate prayer
I stepped inside an old hotel
and saw a girl with wavy hair

Her eyes shined like a memory
of all that lay ahead
and what I feared my destiny
might choose to leave unsaid

There was something so familiar
although we hadn't met
I could hear that cosmic dealer
say go on and place your bets

The lights they quickly flickered
and then broke beyond repair
as she came to me and whispered
time makes dust of all affairs

Her wisdom rose like Noah's ark
above my deluge of self doubt
and as our lips met in the dark
the future was announced

It is by fate that we are led
but you can't resist the signs

Hanging from my final thread
I knew the time was mine

Then together we did ride
on to that Nashville scene
Along with my bewitching bride
I'm chasing every dream

Douglas G. Swezey

#1421 (Miss America Calls the Contact Center)

Miss America phones me at the call center
She is asking so many questions
I can't even keep up
She has so many issues
I don't quite know where to begin
She is rattling them all off so rapidly

I start to take them one by one
But she in on to the next before I can even begin
And they all pile up
While I struggle to take notes on each thing
I want to help
I want to answer all her prayers
I want to have an answer for everything

She has so many children
And each of them are in some kind of trouble
Are they all hers?
Are they orphans she's taken in?
Are they the product of different baby-daddies,
Who knows?

But this one keep getting beat up in the schoolyard
And that one has his lunch money stolen
By the big kids from the swamp
Another won't do her homework
While till another doesn't get enough

Frantic I am to catch up
And she doesn't stop for a breath
I am convinced there is an answer for all
If we could slow down a moment
My computer infrastructure cannot keep up
With all the data being entered

I fear the blue screen of death
Might be coming
So I interrupt her just to ask
If I can place her on hold a moment
She caters to the request
But warns this is urgent
And there isn't time

I signal the supervisor and let them know
This will be a while
And she may wish to get them involved
But I will try to handle this as best I can
When the screen unfreezes
And I take her off hold

I am sorry for the Delay
But make no excuses
And she continues with her fervor
There are so many areas to cover
But I do get her to calm down
And think through each step

Perhaps it needs a reboot
Did you try unplugging the box?
She did it last 4 years ago, and things
Improved, but she is impatient

With all the pixilation
Skewing her view

Well your plan is still active
With no break in coverage
Though she has gone out of network many times
In the past and the coinsurance adds up quickly
It feels overwhelming to her
As if there is no way to ever pay off this tab

The item is on backorder
Would you care for something different?
But *No* she replies, she needs the very item on the bill
And nothing will suffice until it is delivered
I advise it is on the way
And we are doing everything we can to get it

Though I know not everybody is earnestly
Doing their best to push the order through
I let her know that I will escalate the issue
And to please allow 30-45 business days
To process the request
She seems unhappy to wait

But she is thankful for my effort
And she lauds my ear
She commends my spirit
And wishes
To let my supervisor know
I get her to his voicemail to leave a message

I find sometimes people need a shoulder
More than they need immediate resolve

Sometimes uplift than pushback
Reassurance than empty promise
And I, too, want to see her satisfied
As a happy customer

I want her to spread the word about what we do
And how we can best support her endeavours
Innately, all people want to do their best
And be rewarded for doing their job well
Even in the most mundane of tasks
In a grey corner cubicle

Just then, maintenance
Comes to empty my garbage
I am now inspired

Allison Teicher-Fahrbach

Living In a Shell

A solitary beam of light shines within.
The sun casts its rays on a brand new day.
Here I sit,
Patiently awaiting something, anything, to release me from the walls
confining me.
The interior is cumbersome: echoic of a time when I saw beyond these
walls.
Penchant thoughts fulfill the crevices of my mind:
"What if this feeling does not become fulfilled?"
"How will I survive if I exist just within the confines of this shell?"
"What if the light disappears forever?"
The light fades away and I spring forth, grasping at the opportunity that I
cannot pass up this time.
As my head emerges from my shell, my arms and legs follow.
The sky is illuminated with vivid colors: crisp, fading remnants of a beauti-
ful day drifting beyond the horizon.
The enchanting feeling of it all consumes me:
You can hide.
You can hide in the darkness for as long as you desire,
Still, life persists beyond your shell.
Be it turtle or human or anything or one in between,
You, too, can emerge from your shell when you are ready...
These things just take time.
A beam of light shines from within you...
Your soul casts its rays on each brand new day.

Vincent J. Tomeo

Cemetery Poetry Reading

No one cares if I read them my poetry.
It's been a long time since anyone had read a poem to them.
Who cares if my words echo between headstones
Who cares if I sit on wet sod or kick up dirt
I can even scream!

Will you hear me?

I sit on your headstone, knowing you won't care.
Your tombstone reads;

Hello,
Take a seat,
stay awhile.

John Tucker

He Called Her Mag Angelo

In morning light fiercely climbing higher
Her hair ignites as if caught fire

Fading sun less brazen soft dusk graying Shadow turns blazing red to silken
raven
Noticed in this place their space
Only she and burning candles glow

The Bishop thought the Cathedrals ceiling
To be quite high one false move a slip
Queasy feeling she could surely would
Meet her demise

He shouted upward to the rafters
You blazing haired raven haired artist
Who laughs at fear tell me what is the
Compensation you are after

Dear Bishop down below I've requested
For this skillful challenge not a fortune but a Mere six hundred thousand
dollars no less
Am I prepared to go

Artist have you children
Yes Bishop most proud and willing
Three daughters two sons they're on their Own my youngest lad is all I have
while I'm

Here he takes care of the chores at home

Artist I'm rather surprised by that
Your broods been born and raised
Oh Saint Peter we need to chat
This poor woman is being underpaid

Time passed four years plus
As he watched her take
Twelve hundred thousand steps
On each and every blessed truss

Monsignor soon I'll be in my grave
Take this satchel it's what I've saved
See to it she receives a doubled wage
For this magnificent artist with her silvery Hair after all her beauty given

What is fair is fair

J R Turek

Fashion Repeats

Hemlines rise and fall faster than
the national debt, with much more drama.
Skirts flare and flutter to dance in a breezeway
of yesterday then straight and tight enough
to cut knee circulation.

Bell bottoms come and go, peglegs pass in
and out of fashion with trousers, slacks,
palazzos, gauchos, leggings, pedal pushers,
clam diggers, capris
– jeans remain a constant.

Sleeves flounce and wing,
they dolman, they cap, they kimono,
they raglan, they bell, they puff,
they hover between short and long
to settle at three-quarter.

Necklines plunge and pillage with little left
to the imagination; they collar without a leash,
they turtle without a shell, jewel, v-, scoop,
polo, boat, keyhole, sweetheart, they bowtie
and sash with a see-ya sashay and they're gone.

But they'll be back.
They'll all be back
like them or not.

Grandmother admires granddaughter's
new wardrobe – *I had a dress like that*
when I was your age – and the dress
never gets worn but pushed further into
the dark abyss of the closet for years

until the fashion police dictate it's
a nuisance, a waste of space and
with several others articles, relegated
to a black bag and sent to the thrift shop...

where inevitably a savvy fashionista finds them
buys them, treasures to fit the newest trend;
in a few years, she'll clear out her closet
of prints and plaids when solids are all the rage.

Just wait – next season's feature faux pas
are polka dot, patterned, and anything solid
that not's neon.

Don't worry, keep those pink sequin
leopard print lycra pants in your closet –
eventually something old will become
a new trend again.

Rekha Valliappan

thread that journey

granular pinpoints spaghetti snaking,
looking for potholes, to thread the world
together, for jinxed madness to subside;
for colored rain to bleed: limitless

you can trace beginnings, the journey that
circles, consumes itself—an ouroboros
sealed in its own stealth; mannequins in
waxworks. Someone

says death dances in glows, haloed on stars,
on mizzen of weevil kissed xebecs; I have
waited too long, self-flagellating in isolation,
questing to thread

dank effluvium plumes from rotting woodwork;
where masked crowds shred, swallow their tongues
much like jaw-beaked seagulls squirming in anguish
when the straw balance breaks;

they say the worlds adventure will plateau, axil curve.
deep. A lone woman leans out of a tenement window,
crying out to the single red robin pecking a gray puddle
while the quiet beast yaws.

We are the griffon of zero strength, grizzled, smelling of
petrichor, boxed in the gusts of the wild summer billows;
endless different strains scurrying over latticed surfaces,
trailing colored contrails stretched, mixed—

Anne Wagenbrenner

When We're Young

I open my front door, and you fly in, a blur of small beating wings;
You look newly fledged.
So easy to stumble into danger, when we're young.
You fly to the top of the bookcase, and when you stop flying, I see that you're
a wren.
Sofia, my cat, has smelled you, or heard you, and is climbing up to your perch.
You take off from the bookcase in the nick of time.
Sofia tails you, then leaps into the air, catching you in her mouth like a
Frisbee.
My heart now does its own leap; I don't want you to be hurt, or die.
With you in her mouth, Sofia streaks up the stairs. I follow.
Upstairs, Sofia crouches on the carpet, you still in her mouth.
I put my hand on the back of her neck, and say, "Let go of the bird."
Lucky for you, she does, dropping you into my hand.
I then walk back down the stairs, holding you gently.
You're very, very still, but your eyes are open. You seem unharmed, though
shocked.
I look and look at your brand-new wren feathers, like jewels in many shades
of brown and yellow, and at your eyes looking back at me, sometimes
shocked, sometimes curious.
I go into my front yard and lay you gently on the grass, hoping you'll fly off
unaided.
And you do.

Margarette Wahl

When my "Angel" Arrived

An unexpected distraction
came one night.
I was there letting go of Lucy.
Allowing my pet to no longer suffer
release her from pain.

A car pulled up beside mine.
Arguments erupted from humans with something small
inside a cardboard Amazon box.

The Vet Tech held her up, legs sprawled out
"We don't take it in strays."

My heart saw her black and white tuxedo resemblance
to Mia.
Then her leg deformities reminded me of Harry.
Her dark start and resilience was that of Lemmy.
She had a white fur innocence,
that told me Lucy brought her here.

Without hesitation I accepted her.
I rescued an angel and that would be her name.
In a time of pandemic dilemmas and sadness all around.
We both received answered prayers.

I found peace
inside the box of someone else's
unwanted distraction.

Herb Wahlsteen

Intellectual Beauty and Hungry Humans

Today, Adam's sitting on a swing in
Sun Park. Because it's Saturday,
most of Orange County's lead-gray
smog will lie latent until Monday.

Rain raged all week but
finally grants a respite today.
Only harmless, white cumulus
clouds drift a great distance

away: over Arizona, it
seems. East rest the
San Gabriel Mountains. They
lie far above and beyond

Orange County. They're covered with
a thick, white Afghan of bright-white
snow. The snow has almost the same
white shade as the clouds.

Normally, because of the strong smog
that chokes the sky and all below it,
those mountains can't be seen. This
Saturday, however, it is deep asleep.

It will reawaken fully on Monday,
but, today, it hasn't smothered and
buried the sky above and around Orange
County. Lowering his gaze away from

the sublime, Adam turns around:
toward Anaheim. His visionary vision
returns immediately to the mountain
snow, snow-white clouds, white-hot

noon sun, and pale-white
noon moon. Their beauty is
well balanced in a powder-
blue sky. After a while, he

decides to go home. It's lunch
time. He turns completely around.
He sees the street and
people rushing back and

forth in cars literally spewing
poisons. Beyond the street, farther
west, are tall, soot-stained
buildings. "We people sure

have limitations," he sighs while
climbing into his car. He starts it,
then hurries home, hungrily lusting
lunch.

James P. Wagner (Ishwa)

Grandpa's Advice

Have you ever watched the movie *Home Alone*?
Macaulay Culkin, early 90's sensation
A hilarious movie…
Containing a few things that were perhaps
Not so secretly,
Not meant for children.

Like that zipline, out the back bedroom window
To the tree house…
An insurance nightmare to be sure
But to a kid, looks so, so fun
I wanted one…

Whereas any responsible parent would say no…
My Grandmother said, sure!
And rigged up a make-shift zipline for me
Between two trees in her backyard
Using some kind of clothing line,
And a broken handle of a snow shovel.
Just perfect for my 5-year-old imitation
Of Kevin Mccallister

So, I climb up the step ladder
That my grandma provided for me
Took hold of the handles and
Woooooosh!
Zip, zip, zip down the zipline…

BAM, right into the other tree.
I fell to the ground, and start crying.

"Hey!!" my Grandpa said his stern voice
Commanding my attention,
And putting an immediate halt to my sobbing.
"Get up, walk it off, do it again right..."
I wiped my tears.
"That's what will make you feel better!"

Shocked back to seriousness,
I went back to the zipline, and did it again.
This time, able to brace myself,
Control my movements,
And not smash face first into the tree.

How easy it would have been...
To sit there crying,
For who knows how long...
Focusing on the bruises,
And the failure.

In the thirty years since then,
There have been plenty of times,
Plenty of more serious injuries...
Physically...
Emotionally...
Plenty of worse failures...
But I've always done my best,
To remember those few words
Of wisdom.
"Get up, walk it off, do it again right,"
And true to Grandpa's advice...

Every time I follow that mantra…
No matter how bad it is,
I feel better.

Jillian Wagner

When Autumn Comes

I came to you one summer.
I remained with you for years,
learning, understanding, getting better.
Soon, I became the one you relied on,
the one to solve the problems,
the one to perform miracles,
and the one to clean up the messes others made.
You depend on me.
But I wonder,
what will you do when I am gone?
Because when the autumn leaves fall, I will be gone.
When autumn comes, I will no longer be there to help you.
What will you do now?
Who will you depend on?
Because, truth be told,
I don't think you'll know what to do.
But when autumn comes,
you won't have me to fix the problems anymore.
When autumn comes, I will be gone.
What will you do now?

Virginia Walker

Outliving Your Appliances

The drop-in stove no longer available,
thus, to replace requires removing
one cabinet, perhaps more, face-lift
for a kitchen about half as old as you.

The dishwasher is leaking and past
its warranty, no matter how still
shiny the stainless exterior, the
rot and rust erode one corner lip.

The video camera may not work with
the new computer which you are still
learning to use and you have yet
to get the High-8s transferred to DVDs.

You lucked up on the washing machine.
During Covid a masked man repaired
the stalled machine while still under
warranty. Clean sheets, clean masks.

At night you listen to the refrigerator
hoping it keeps humming and the phone,
out once for a month, thanks to PSEGLI,
keeps contact with the entropic world.

You do not want a new stove, just this one
repaired, but it would need removal,
overhaul, fabricated parts, a bespoke
proposition, one you cannot afford.

And we have not gotten to the super-
structure over all—the house itself—
there seems to be some mold, leaks
I know and no money for reconstruction.

Aging is not a sometimes thing, but it is
hit and miss, hitting mostly when least
expected or desired, and not missing
a trick in getting under your skin.

George Wallace

In Youth Or Any Age, Even in Time of Plague

To know your secret, to declassify you, to feel you rush
like a fine claret in the veins of my arms, or flicker like
candleflame in the thick of my neck, to burn with the
anguish of desire, to possess you and be possessed;

To tender your weaknesses and bring virtue to its knees,
to breach you like a ship breaches a cold dark sea, you!
who are all else to me and a bulwark to oblivion, you! all
that defines me, my lips and breasts like honeycombs,
my beard and belly and hips, victim to your kisses;

To be love's casualty which does not happen by degrees,
but by overwhelming surprise like Norse ships, fierceness
of a summer squall; your misplaced caresses which subdue
me, your aura which is measureless,

Your sidelong glances which are child's play in the school
yard, your logic which is embarassing, syllogisms scrawled
on a blackboard -- lawless, not even mathematical, irrefutable;

O to be yours, lover, eagerly, yieldingly, heir to nothing and everything,
the boldness and the ready grief;

To be rooted in you, like new grass in fresh soil, to take what taint
and livelihood may be taken from you, the very plasma of you,
flesh and bone, replenished for the taking;

These are love's fingerprints, mark my dna;
these are love's inconquerables and esoterics,
in youth or any age, even in time of plague;

Call it inheritance, call it god, call it inevitability,
we are heaven, i am yours

Marq Wells

Metamorphosis
For Bill A.

At the funeral home
each visitor who has
arrived to remember
Julia, shuffles down the isle -
smiling respectfully as if
to absolve themselves
from their own personal grief
and the revelation
of their own mortality

And after the Father has chanted his peace,
emanating and incense, wealth and welfare
for the loved ones and for the Great Ecumenical,
the visitors disperse and you alone
are left to grieve,

never quite prepared
to deal with the specter of death
as you suddenly grow up all over again,
twisted vine amongst the sharp
brambles and needy weeds
out here in the expanse
of this island   Paumanok.

Then
I am distracted by a vagabond troupe

of arch angels whom beckon you with
brand new mutant trumpets
that rip a shimmering hole
through heaven's gates
to a degree
that gets GOD really …

miffed but God knows
it's is not your time yet

as all these angels gently weep
because they really want to jam with you
and your guitar which sparks my own revelation
that I am never packing any gig bags
to bring all my crap with me
once I make that great leap,

that holy Jump over the great divide.

That metamorphosis back
into some creature who's name is
always on the tip of my tongue
but with whom I will never become intimate

never appreciate until it's too late
for me to lift and drop a question on my plate
or even object.

as angels will have their way
or so it seems with each of us
In due time for us to return to coda
And continue through the great reprise.

Jack Zaffos

A House I Can Get Out Of

My story gets stuck in the way.
I am in a web,
entangled in a box
I can't get out of.

Persona persona persona,
A house I can't get out of,
where I am just a charade.

When confronted face to face
I lapse back into that dance
with the fancy footwork,
treading softly,
not to upset the gate keepers.

When the web takes hold of the throat,
my song cannot be sung.

Summon the gatekeepers.
tell them to let me out.
Don't they know that it is imperative
that I speak here?

Don't they know it's a diminishment
of the song of the world?
There is something that needs
to be said here,

beyond the constraints of proper,
beyond the constraints of
self-definition.

This is a wake-up call,
one that's comes from
the roots in the soil
from a tree of light
that can no longer
be constrained.

Steven Zaluski

The Girl

I always wonder
What she's wearing
If she's caring
About me...
We never know in this dance of romance...
How the plot thickens
My heart quickens
When she laughs at my quips
Our separate ships
Collide in the night
It feels just right...
As the voyagers sail on...
Making dreams come true
Chasing away my blues...

Thomas Zampino

Writing Poetry

The hardest part about writing poetry, at least sometimes, is not knowing how it will end and how I will get there.

It usually flows pretty easily at first – like that time I told you about the hardest part about writing poetry.

Then I might fumble a bit in the middle as I buy some time, looking for something clever to say while trying to avoid becoming self-referential.

And then comes the ending.

It usually takes even me by surprise.

Especially today, since I've been daydreaming this whole time, vividly recalling my younger days as a pilot flying solo for the US Post Office in Omaha.

Back in the 1940s.

The decade before I was born.

Donna Zephrine

Faith is

Faith is trust and respect
Faith is love and understanding
Faith is caring and sharing
Faith is strength and conviction
Faith is hope for a better tomorrow
Faith is empathy and sympathy
Faith is giving and receiving
Faith is all good things that life has to offer

Lewis Zimmerman

To Jenny In The Mid-Day Class

In my Decade
the pink ink would have earned you a zero
and a sharp reprimand from Mrs. Kuhlenberg
for the daisies and ballet slippers
and little hearts surrounding your nickname
scrawled repeatedly on the assignment sheet
while the most irritatingly-smitten young swain in the back row
would see them scribbled dancingly down the margin
and be charmed
as I am now
at the sweet assurance
that girls still dream

About the Authors

Lloyd Abrams is a long-time Freeport resident, is a retired high school teacher and administrator and is an avid recumbent bicycle rider and long-distance walker. Lloyd has been writing short stories for over thirty years and poems for almost a dozen years. His works have been published in more than three dozen anthologies and publications. www.lbavha.com/write

Sharon Anderson has been published in many international and local anthologies, has been nominated for a Pushcart prize, and has four publications of her own poetry with a fifth to be released soon. She serves on the advisory boards of theNassau County Poet Laureate Society, and the Bards Initiative.

William H. Balzac is the author of two books of poetry, "The Wind Shall Hear My Words," and "The Stars Will Speak Them." He also has been a contributor to The Bards Annual (2019 & 2020), The Suffolk County Poetry Review (2019 & 2020), and two Chapbooks (published by Local Gems Press), "The Same Page," (2020) and "Morning Light" (2021). William resides in Deer Park, Long Island.

Christine A. Barbour is a Queens, NY resident. She is a direct descendent of Adam Mott, a founding family of Hempstead, NY. Christine has an MFA from Sarah Lawrence College and a BA from Queens College. In 2010, she founded **Iron Horse Poetry**, a free craft class and workshop. She facilitates its Facebook page www.facebook.com/IronHorsePoetry/. Christine has been published in *Writer's Digest*, *Performance Poets Association*, *Rhino*, the *Nassau County Poet Laureate Society*, *Bards Annual*, among others.

Patricia Z. Beach is pursuing her passion for writing after a diverse career in transportation management. Publications include PPA Literary Review (vol. 21), Bards Annual 2016 and Chicken Soup for the Soul (2019). A recipient of

Long Island Literary Arts prose award (2019 2nd place), Patricia holds a BA in English from St. John's University and a MS in Construction Management from NYU. She is a member of the Farmingdale Creative Writing Group.

Joe Beck is a freelance writer and educator who got his start after he sold a story about his African safari adventure when he was 19. He's since written, co-written and ghost-written 12 books, 10 plays and hundreds of articles from banana ripening rooms to medical murder mystery thrillers to a family drama, starring Brian Dennehy and Austin Pendleton. He's accepted an invite to join the Yale Writers' Workshop, taught writing at Kingsborough College in Brooklyn and teaches English on Long Island. He's a proud member of The Authors Guild and The Dramatists Guild.

Antonio Bellia (Madly Loved) A renaissance man. He has traveled many paths. A man of deep sentiment drawn to the performing arts. He has performed as a dancer, actor throughout his lifetime. From a very young age he was compelled to express his emotions and experiences in the form of poetry. They have been shared through his passionate readings in the N.Y. area. Antonio is known by many as Madly Loved.

Robyn Bellospirito is an artist and writer, having recently published her first book, "Memoirs of a Little Ghost: Selected Writings from 2002-2015." Aside from her art and writing, Robyn is a tanpura player, a tarot card reader, and a shamanic practitioner. She resides in Huntington Station, NY. For further information please visit: www.robynbellospirito.com

Selina Benson is a native New Yorker. Her work has been published in an anthology by the National Library of Poetry. She is in the process of publishing a collection of her poetry. She currently resides in a small Long Island community with her two sons.

Thérèse M. Craine Bertsch, DSW, LCSW a mother and grandmother has a long history as a clinical supervisor, program/staff development. She was a pioneer in HIV/AIDS programs. At 81 she continues this work at Project

Safety Net, NY for clients in need. Through poetry she gives voice to her questions hoping to console others.

Renee Bess was born, raised and continues to live in her childhood home in Hempstead,NY. She holds a BFA in Theatre and Dance from Pratt Institute. Renee finds writing short stories and poems therapeutic.

Lorene Vorbach Bossong, a life long poet, has focused her recent retirement from education on developing her writing. Her work has been published in a variety of anthologies including Bards Annual 2011, Poets to Come, Oberon, Corona Global Lockdown and Nassau County Poet Laureate Review. When she's not writing, Lorene spends time with her family, especially her grand-children. She lives in Hicksville with her husband.

Alex Edwards-Bourdrez is the author of three chapbooks of poetry: *Transformations*, *Tapestries*, and *Psalms for the Common Era*, all published by Local Gems Press. His poetry has won prizes in contests across Long Island and is included in various anthologies. He lives in Northport.

Michael Brozinsky is a retired mathematics teacher who lives in Central Islip with his wife Susan. He likes to reminisce about growing up in Brooklyn and take photos of nature. He never wrote a poem before Jan 8,2021 but has now written 80.

Rich Buley-Neumar has been writing for most of his life, everything from poems to plays, from essays to press releases, and everything in between. Although not professionally published thus far, he continues to share his creativity in any way he can. Rich is the assistant director of an adoption agency specializing in placing young teens, and lives in Amityville with his husband and one of his five sons.

Alice Byrne is a clinical social worker in practice in Huntington,New York. She is a mother,grandmother and mother- in-law.she began writing poetry as a child.

Louisa Calio is an internationally published, award winning poet and a photo artist. Her works have been translated into Sicilian, Italian, Russian, Korean and Tagrinya. She won 1st Prize for "Bhari", City of Messina, Sicily (2013) a finalist, poet laureate Nassau County(2013), Director, Poets Piazza, Hofstra, 12 years, Winner "Il Parnasso" internationale 1st Prize (2017) and Words of Gold (2016) (2021) Canicatti, Sicily, Connecticut Commission of the Arts Grant for Writers, honored at Columbia/Barnard as A Feminist who changed American 2nd wave. Her latest book **Journey to the Heart Waters** published by Legas Press (2014). See: http://en.wikipedia.org/wiki/Louisa_Calio

Carlo Frank Calo, grandson of Sicilian immigrants, husband, father, grand-father, born in East Harlem, grew up in the Bronx projects, retired on Long Island. Enjoys fishing, bicycling, poker, working part-time counseling TBI survivors, babysitting his grandchildren, writing eclectically. Publications: Hippocampus Magazine, The Copperfield Review, High Coupe 2014, Down in the Dirt Magazine, Local Gems Press: Suffolk County Poetry Review 2018, Bards Annual 2017- 2020, No Distance Between Us, Walt Whitman's Bicen-tennial Poets to Come, We Are Beat-National Beat Poetry Foundation.

Lee Crace Cannella, B.S., M.A., has used the arts to enhance the lives of those who suffer from special needs. As a Therapeutic Recreation Specialist at the Long Island State Veterans Home, she enabled disabled veterans to ex-press themselves through writing, poetry and wheelchair dance. During her employment at a school for the hearing impaired, she taught students how to dance while choreographing sign language into movement. Now retired, her memories and life experiences find their way into her poetry. As a wife, mother and grandmother, living on Long Island since 1963, has planted her, a city person, into suburban richness.

LynneRose Cannon hails from Wilmington, Vermont, now, but she lived all of her life on Long Island before her recent move. She's working on a poetry collection and has written two novels.

Gloria Cassandra-Jainchill was born in Long Island City and grew up in East Meadow, Long Island, and still maintains her Long Island accent though she left many years ago for a job in Hartford, CT. Gloria has published several poetry books, her last being My Glastonbury Poetry, a gathering of pictures and poetry about where she lives today. Gloria has strong roots in Long Island with several siblings, and many nieces, nephews, and cousins living between East Hampton and Long Island City.

Cate Chirico makes her home in the beautiful seaside town of Northport with her kids and furry friends . She enjoys hiking in Nature, taking photos and painting . More of her musings can be found on FB Insta and Fineartamerica.com

Anne Coen is a retired special education teacher. She has featured at Sip This, The Bellmore Bean, Bellmore Public Library, Oceanside Library, and the Oceanside Gazebo. Publishing credits include the PPA Literary Review, Bards Annual, Thirteen Days of Halloween, Poets4Paris, Rhyme and Punishment, and The Hands We Hold.

Joe Coen is an abstract artist and the other half of a poetic duo with his wife Anne. He is the father of a free spirit and an Airforce Sergeant. Active with of the Performance Poets Association, Poets in Nassau, and The Bards Initiative, he has featured at Sip This and the Bellmore Memorial Library. His work has been published on the Poets4Paris website and book, in *Balance 2016* and appeared in multiple issues of the *PPA Literary Review* and *Bards Annual*. He was awarded First Runner Up in the Long Island Light Poetry Competition.

Jamie Ann Colangelo is a Christian, living on Long Island. She is the mother of twins, Liane and Christopher, now adults. She is the author of *The Lion and The Lamb Within – A Poetic Expression of Love and Faith* and *From The Father's Heart - A Book of Poems and Suggested Gifts To Inspire, Encourage and Bless Those in Your Circle of Influence.* She found her passion for poetry at the age of 12 and now enjoys using her gifts and talents to share God's love and encourage others on life's journey.

Lorraine Conlin is the Nassau County Poet Laureate Emeritus (2015-2017) Vice-president of the NCPLS and Events Coordinator for PPA. She hosts weekly poetry workshops on Zoom since the beginning of quarantine. Her poems have been published nationally and internationally in anthologies and literary reviews.

Nancy Connolly has been journaling for over 35 years. She finds great joy in the placement of select of words to create an image or emotion with the least words.

Shakira Croce is a writer living in Lynbrook, New York. Her debut poetry collection, Leave It Raw (Finishing Line Press, 2020), has been featured on the New Books Network and Mom Egg Review, and includes poems that explore the nuances of sexuality, motherhood, the arts, and ambition, speaking to relationships' potential to hurt and heal. Croce's poetry has been featured in several literary magazines and journals, including the New Ohio Review, Pilgrimage Press, Ducts, pioneertown, Permafrost Magazine, and Shark Reef. Croce holds a Bachelor of Arts from Sarah Lawrence College and a Master's in Public Administration from Pace University.

Victoria Crosby has been Poet Laureate of the City of Gen Cove since 1994 and has written for many magazines and newspapers including Per-Verse, a weekly poetry column of political satire, for the now defunct Long Island Press. Ms Crosby has been a reporter for The North Shore Leader since 2004, and was a writer and poet for Brookville Living and 25A Magazines. Her three poetry books of political satire are available on Amazon.

Michele Cuomo was born in White Plains, NY but came to Huntington Station in her first year, and grew up in Islip Hamlet. She returned to Islip as an adult for a few short years and is presently enjoying life in Florida with her husband Paul and receiving Long Island family members in the winter months. She recently published her first chapbook, BURN through Local Gems. michelecuomo@hotmail.com

Paula Curci produces *Calliope's Corner - The Place Where Poets and Songwriters Meet and What's the Buzz* ®, on Radio Hofstra University. She co-founded the poetry band *The Acoustic Poets Network* ™ and performs using an aesthetic she developed called Posics ™. Paula has won several awards for her poetry, broadcasts and counseling education.

Megan Dausch is a writer and accessibility Specialist living on Long Island. She makes her home with her husband and guide dog. Her work has appeared in "The Tishman Review," "Third Wednesday," "Breath and Shadow," and "The Promethean."

Max Dawson works full-time with adults with mental illness. But Dawson is better defined by his interests in The Civil War, The old west, trains of that era, Victorian science fiction and horror, and most importantly, writing. He has been published in Bard's Annual Poetry Anthology, he has also been published in The Beat Generation Poetry Anthology, and he is writing a book.

Jeanne D'Brant is a holistic physician and biology professor who leads annual field trips to the rainforests of Central & South America. Author of the nonfiction book *Heartlands of Islam*, Jeanne has been published in many scientific and alternative medicine journals. She loves to wander the world and her poetry is inspired by her travels and nature.

Debbie De Louise is a reference librarian at a public library. She's the author of eleven novels including a cozy mystery series. Her poems are also featured in the Nassau County Voices In Verse 2020 anthology and the 2020 Bards Annual. Her stories and poetry also appear in the Red Penguin Collection anthologies. She lives on Long Island with her husband, daughter, and three cats. https://debbiedelouise.com

Sharon Dua is a volunteer for a non-profit organization, New Beginnings Community Center for Traumatic Brain Injury in Medford. In her free time, she likes movies & writing children's stories and poems (anywhere from serious to funny to all about life) She also likes to spend time baking, crafting, and spending time with her family.

Michael Duff was born in New York and raised in Queens. He is and always will be a Ramones Fan. He moved to Long Island a little more than three years ago and has been living in Freeport for close to three years. He makes a living as a journalist and photographer.

Madelyn Edelson has always written poetry, even during the 28 years spent teaching English and Humanities at Oceanside Senior High School.

Bonnie Ellman is a poet and freelance writer from Great Neck, NY. She has been writing for over five years and also took part in The Writer's colony at The New School. She holds a bachelor's degree in history and a master's degree in Modern Literature from Royal Holloway, University of London. She now lives in Forest Hills, NY.

Melissa E. Filippelli is a native Long Islander who writes because she must. Every hard thing in her life has given her a deep, clear, and tender voice that others can relate to. You can find more of her writing in various publications including Suffolk County Poetry Review 2020 edition, Bards Annual 2019 and 2020, and Poets to Come, an anthology dedicated to Walt Whitman.

Adam D. Fisher is the author of poetry, stories and liturgy. In addition to publishing many poems in journals and magazines, he has published four books of poetry: *Rooms, Airy Rooms* (Writers Ink, Cross Cultural Communications and Behrman House), *Dancing Alone* (Birnham Wood/ LI Quarterly), *Enough to Stop the Heart* (Writers Ink) and *Hanging Out With God* (Writers Ink.) He was Poetry Editor (2006-2014) of the CCAR Journal, the Journal of the Central Conference of American Rabbis.

Denise Marie Fisher has lived for 42 years in a home she had built, by the Great South Bay. She has been involved in many poetry workshops and groups, including Poetry Tag Group- which she helped create and run for ten years. She has been published in several analogies and newsletters both online and in print. She prefers the sonnet form and has written hundreds of sonnets.

M. Frances Garcia, M.A., is a freelance journalist and contemplative poet and photographer. She is also an adjunct professor of English at Suffolk Community College in Selden, NY; and holds a Master of Social Work (MSW) from Fordham University in New York. She believes in the inspirational and healing power of Nature to promote peace and joy in life.

George S. George is the son of Cypriot immigrants who came to America in the 1920s. He was born in Brooklyn, NY, and as a child lived in Virginia, North Carolina and New Jersey. He was graduated from Rutgers University in 1963, taught English and eventually went into advertising. He now lives on Long Island with his wife, Joan.

Gina Giannetti is a life-long Long Islander with a deep passion for literature. She has been writing poetry and fantasy fiction since her high school days. Writing is her favorite way to express herself, and sharing that expression is her favorite way to spend her time.

After writing poetry for more than half a century, **Tina Lechner Gibbons** was first published in the Bards Annual 2019. Since then she has been published in several Local Gems anthologies, and also published her own chapbook titled "Down by the River". She continues to write poems and has started a compilation of essays & stories based on memories of her life.

D. Dolson Gregory is an unpublished writer with unpublished thoughts in a body of unpublished experience. Having garnered attention for a public painting or two, he squandered opportunity and devoted most of his working life assisting a far more recognized artist, one who, like the former assistant presented before you, changed his name to find his fame, then so far, unlike the star before you now, changed the course of art history. Today, from a Hampton in Long Island, he runs that artist's Foundation.

Aaron Griffin is an alleged copywriter and novelist who worked full time in a warehouse club outside of Charlotte, NC and now lives in Ohio. Originally from Long Island, NY. Aaron loves trains, pinwheels, windmills, and useless statistics about Japanese cartoon monsters. His favorite activities include spinning things, playing with imaginary animals, shaking things, and watching ice melt.

Marie Griffin is a bard who lives in Spartanburg, SC. She spent part of her childhood in Long Island New York. She has recently published fiction in Freedom Fiction and other small press journals. She enjoys reading, walking, and spending time with her three brilliant felines.

Daryel Groom has had numerous poems and short stories published in college literary magazines such as Nassau Community College *This is Big Paper* and Molloy College's *Curiouser Curiouser*. In addition, she has published articles in the Nassau Community College *Vignette*. Additionally, she has had the following poems published "Phantoms" in the 2019 edition of Nassau County *Voices in Verse* and *" Archangel of Peace"* in *Bards Annual* 2020 edition. Furthermore, she contributed to an online publication focusing on ancestry with a piece entitled "My American Ancestry". She is an animal activist who volunteers at Posh Pets in Long Beach, New York. She currently teaches high school English & Math at a Juvenile Detention Center in Nassau County.

Maureen Hadzick - Spisak is a retired Reading and English Teacher, an award winning poet, and the author of two poetry books: *A Bite of the Big Apple* and *Yesterday I Was Young*. Her poems have appeared in over fifty anthologies. She is a member of the Bards Initiative and the Farmingdale Creative Writing Group.

Geneva Hagar lives in Melville, NY. She has a BA in Fine Arts from Stony Brook University. Geneva has published three books, The Folk Art Poet,Moon Flowers and The Silver Tree. She has been honored by being accepted in the Bards Annual 2019, 2020, The Long Island Quarterly 2019 and the Suffolk County Poetry Review 2019.

Nick Hale is a founder and current Vice President of the Bards Initaitive. He is also the founder of NoVA Bards and the Northern Virginia Poetry Group. Formerly both a literal and metaphorical hat collector, these days, Nick only collects metaphorical hats. He is a partner, publisher, editor, and author with Local Gems Press and has worked on several anthologies including the best-selling *Sound of Solace*. In addition to writing, editing, and performing poetry, Nick enjoys teaching poetry and has given several seminars, panels, and workshops on various poetic topics. In his own poetry, he often enjoys humor and experimenting with different styles, which may make him seem, at times, like he has yet to find his voice. Along with James P. Wagner, Nick co-authored *Japanese Poetry Forms: A Poet's Guide*. He is the author of *Broken Reflections* and three upcoming chapbooks which, he claims haven't been published yet only because he's too busy working on books that are not his.

Sylvia Harnick is a member of the National League of American Pen Women admitted as poet and mixed media artist. Her poems have been published in PPA Literary Review, Toward Forgivenes, Whispers and Shouts and in many local venues. Her creative process in poetry and painting is similar, using imagery, metaphor and enigma.

Robert L. Harrison has had his creative work published in over 80 books. These books include his historic research, photo covers, photographs and poetry. He was awarded the George M. Estabrook Award from Hofstra University.

George Held's work has appeared in Blue Unicorn, Spring, Transference, and Two Cities Review, among other periodicals, and has received eleven Pushcart Prize nominations. Among his 22 books is the poetry chapbook Second Sight (2019); his forthcoming book, The Lucky Boy, collects nine of his short stories.

Diane Hill was born and raised on Long Island. She still lives here as do her children and grandchildren. Diane has been writing poetry since she was a teenager. She finds poetry to be a creative and cathartic way to express her emotions...the good, the bad, and the ugly
.

Arnie Hollander published a quarterly magazine, **Grassroot Reflections,** prior to the arrival of coronavirus and the Great Shutdown. He has poems in various anthologies including Paumanok Interwoven. He has poems and short stories in the online magazine, **Bewildering Stories** and keeps a blog at www.arnieh.webs.com.

Kevin Holmes: a simple family man from Brooklyn to Kings Park. Had a grandmother who taught him love.

Idorenyin (Eee-doh-ren-yin) is a New Yorker and poetry lover who has been writing poetry off and on for years. It was during the pandemic that Idorenyin resumed writing poetry consistently because she found this helped her and those around her deal with all that was going on.

Maria Iliou is an autistic artist, poet, actress, director, producer, advocate, and host. Maria's been published in *Perspectives, Bards Annual 2011-2016,* and *Rhyme and PUNishment.* Maria is host for *Athena Autistic Artist*, which airs on public access tv and hosts the radio show, *Mind Stream The Movement of Poetry and Music.*

Evie Ivy is a dancer/poet in the NYC poetry circuit. She is the host of one of the longest running poetry events, the Green Pavilion Poetry Event, held in Brooklyn usually on the last Wednesdays. *The Platinum Moon*, (Dark Light Publishing), her latest book, can be purchased through Amazon.

Jay Jii Poetic thespian. Writer. Composer. Artist. Classical guitarist. Bohemian. Adventurer. Romantic. Like that…

Edward John went into quarantine and needed a "thing" to do. He started writing a poem a day. He's written 371 so far.

Amie Kachinoski is the proud author of her first chapbook "Walking Contradiction". When she is not writing poetry, songs for her guitar, or children's books, she is a trained yoga teacher for seniors and uses her newfound freedom to navigate this unscripted world.

Rorie Kelly is a singer, songwriter, poet, tarot reader, and ladybeast from Sound Beach NY. Her life's mission is to use her art to inspire you (in particular!) to love yourself fiercely, and to honor and celebrate fellow wonderful weirdos who feel they don't fit into the mainstream. She has a weekly livestream called Monday Night Muses where she features original music, poetry and general shenanigans. Find her online by typing "rorie kelly" into your favorite social media or music streaming site.

Daniel Basil Kerr, CPA, Ph.D. is a cross-cultural consultant focused on helping people and organizations work across borders. He teaches graduate classes accounting at St. Joseph's College and is also a licensed lay minister in the Episcopal church. His poems about religion, politics, history, and "growing up in Asharoken in the 1960s" have been published in Bards Annual, Suffolk County Poetry Review, Performance Poets Association, Beat Generation, and other anthologies.

Laura Kolitsopoulos works in the food industry. She describes cooking as an art. Laura is a native New Yorker. She enjoys spending time with her family and enjoys writing poetry.

Carissa Kopf is an inspiring poet who has published a number of poems, along with her first poetry book called, Coffee, Wine, and the Magic of Words. Carissa also is the author of a novella called, Time For Me. When not teaching, her fingers dance across the keyboard creating more poems and stories. Carissa enjoys writing at coffee shops, beaches, parks, and or right on her patio where she loves to garden.

Michael Krasowitz writes his poetry at the most inopportune moments. Usually an idea comes to him in the middle of the night and knows, with utmost certainty, that if he does not get up just then and write it down it will be lost. He wishes he could just press a button on his forehead and everything would just be recorded.

Mindy Kronenberg is a widely published poet and writer, professor of writing and the arts at SUNY Empire State College, and editor of *Oberon* poetry magazine. Her work has been featured in art installations and video projects, and she has read online for *Creative Expressions* arts forum, *Poetry Street*, *Second Saturdays* poetry series, and *The Eric Norcross Podcast*.

Joan F. Kuchner, Ph.D. Retired Director., Child & Family Studies, Dept. of Psychology, Stony Brook Univ. honored for her teaching & academic writing on infancy, children's play & intergenerational issues, now enjoys writing poetry on these same themes as well as spending time playing with her four grandchildren. Her poems have been published in *Lilith, Oberon Poetry Magazine, Bard's Annual,* and the *Nassau County Poet Laureate Society Review.*

Tara Lamberti is a psychic and poet who lives in Head of the Harbor with her beloved Golden Retriever, Chewbacca.

Billy Lamont is a multimedia poetry performer who has performed on national television a number of times, including MTV and Joe Franklin Show, toured and performed with rock festivals such as Lollapalooza, and appeared on major radio stations across the U.S. He has three books of poetry and nine album CD/digital download releases. His latest album *Eulogy:Flowers For The Living* was just released and his latest book *Words Ripped From A Soul Still Bleeding: Poems For The Future Edition* is available at Barnes And Noble and Amazon as a paperback or as an eBook.

Linda Leff Although quietly writing poetry for many years, inclusion in *Bards Annual 2020* has invigorated her passions. Highly motivated to pursue this calling, inspiration can be found in enjoyable moments with family and friends: hikes, archery, fishing or the sights and smells of the seashore. Looking forward to continued participation within Long Island's poetry community.

Eleanor Lerman, the author of numerous award-winning collections of poetry, short stories and novels, is a National Book Award finalist, has received both NEA and Guggenheim fellowships, and was awarded the Lenore Marshall Prize for Poetry from the Academy of American Poets. Her most recent novel, *Watkins Glen* (Mayapple Press), was published in June 2021.

Iris Levin is a retired educator. She writes with open eyes and open heart. Her work has been included in *Whispers and Shouts, Nassau County Poet Laureate Review, Bards Annual, Sounds of Solace, Paumanok:Poems and*

Pictures of Long Island, Performance Poets Literary Review, Corona Anthology, Never Forgotten 100 poets remember 9/11

Stephen Loomis is a Clinical Psychologist, who resides and maintains his private practice in Nassau County, NY. His work has appeared in print and online, and three professionally performed plays. He has a lovely wife and two wonderful sons, none of whom find anything he writes even slightly amusing. (sigh)

Once an executive business woman and innovator, poetry and photography award recipient **Sheri Lynn,** enjoys developing activism and creative insights expressed through poetry, stories, and photography -- proof each of us may transform! Sheri launched her first poetry and photography chapbook "Nature's Breath", accompanying notecards and website BreatheInsights.com in 2019. Sheri is grateful for encouragement from family, friends, the writing community and all who have published her other works: *Ms. Magazine, Chicken Soup for the Soul-Listen to Your Dreams, The Odyssey magazine, NCPLS, PPA, DBP, Bards, TNSPS, The 911 Memorial Museum* and more.

Cristian Martinez is a 14-year-old 9th-grade student at Connetquot High School and award winning poet. He has been published in Bards Annual 2018, 2019 and 2020, PPA 23rd Annual Literary Review, Suffolk County Poetry Review 2019 and 2020, Mankh's Haiku Calendar for 2019 and 2020 and the Long Island Quarterly. Cristian won first place in the Princess Ronkonkoma Awards competition for his poetry and prose submissions in 2018 and 2019, PPA 1st place for a haiku submitted, and 1st in the Mid-Island Y 2019 Contest. He was awarded for his poem, "Glimpse of Tomorrow" with recognition as the Grand Champion for the Walt Whitman Birthplace Contest and published in their anthology. *Glimpse of Tomorrow* is Cristian's first book that has now been published in 2021. He has been mentored by Robert Savino for the past three years which has helped Cristian fine-tune his craft. Cristian also loves to play soccer.

Kathleen Lynch McCarrey grew up in Freeport one of 14 children. Moved to FL , and back to raise 2 children in Holtsville. Now living with husband in GA. Mother of 2. Grandmother of seven. Avid reader, and occassional writer. Honored to have been chosen.

Rosemary McKinley is an eclectic writer who has had poetry, short stories, as well as articles published. Her three historical books: 101 Glimpses of the North Fork and Islands, the Wampum Exchange, and Captain Henry Green, a whaler all center on the history of the East End of Long Island, New York. www.rosemarymckinley.com

John F. McMullen, *"johnmac the bard"*, is the Poet Laureate of the Town of Yorktown, NY, a member of the American Academy of Poets, the author of over 2,500 columns and 10 books, a college professor, and a radio host.

Mollie McMullan is a senior in high school who has been writing poetry since 6th grade. Her poetry is an amalgamation of personal experiences and stories she's heard over the years. She hopes to publish her own poetry book one day.

Gene McParland (North Babylon, NY): A graduate from Queens College and possessing graduate degrees from other institutions, Gene has published various research papers *BUT* have always had a passion for poetry and the messages it can convey. His works have appeared in numerous publications, and previous editions of the Bards Annual. He is also the author of Baby Boomer Ramblings, a collection of essays and poetry, and Adult Without, Child Within, poetry celebrating our inner child. Gene also performs in Community Theater and film, mostly home grown original works; and has written several plays.

Heather C. Meehan is a writer, farmer, and educator currently based in Sag Harbor. Her work has appeared in *The Berkshire Edge, Euphoria Magazine, Movement Research Performance Journal,* and *Glacial Erratic.* She received a B.A. from Simon's Rock in 2014.

Lisa Meyer ALL ROADS HOME, ALL ROADS DESTINED and ALL ROADS SHATTERED are Lisa Diaz Meyer's current books of dark short fiction and dark poetry. Readers can also find her work in Nassau County Voices In Verse 2020, Bards Annual 2020, and in several Red Penguin Books publications. She hails from Long Island's south shore. For more information visit www.lisadiazmeyer.com

Lisa Mintz is a multi-media artist in the fields of writing, photography, and pottery. She has led professional development workshops to promote focus and mindfulness through creativity. She is currently working on publishing a book combining her poetry and photography. Lisa lives with her husband in Dix Hills, and is a mother of three and grandmother of two.

Amanda Montoni is a dance teacher, choreographer, and director on Long Island and a co-founder of a theater company in Queens. Throughout her life, writing has always been another outlet to express herself and she is lucky to be featured in multiple anthologies. Her self-published poetry collections are available at www.amandamontoni.com. Her intent is for readers to find companionship in her work.

CR Montoya has written a series of children's stories narrated by Papa The Happy Snowman; self-publishing, on Amazon, began in May 2020. He is published in several poetry journals. His poem, titled Procrastinator in Chief, was published in the 10th Annual Long Island Bards Anthology in 2020. CR has a curious mind and is a student of nature. Running on trails is a source of inspiration. He is a lifelong Long Islander and lives in Nassau County with his wife and three dogs. **Like Papa on Facebook at papathehappysnowman**

Dianne Moritz writes adult poetry and poems/picture books for kids. Her book, 1, 2, 3 BY THE SEA, is a bestseller. This is her first attempt at rap.

Sean Morris comes from Brooklyn and has spent more than half his life living in Long Island. He's had a hard time, but he strives to see beauty in the world.

Mary Sheila Morrissey grew up in Kings Park. Since 2016, she has published five books of her poetry. Her poems have been read and reviewed on a Hofstra University's radio program and included in a Michigan art exhibition. Mary lives in Brentwood.

Ian Murdock lives in Northport, Long Island and is presently semi-retired. He is not a poet; he is just a guy who fell in love.

Edward Nardoza is an editor and writer based in Hampton Bays, Long Island. He has edited and contributed to various international publications, most recently serving as Editor in Chief of Fairchild Media's WWD.

Marsha M Nelson is an award-winning poet, playwright, and screenwriter. Her poem "I Thought It Was Love" won the Nassau County Poet Laureate Society 2016 contest. In 2018, she was nominated for the Blue Light Press Pushcart Prize for her poem, "Hairpins and a Box of Chocolates" and was a third prize recipient in the Super Poem Contest at Walt Whitman Birthplace.

George H Northrup is a psychologist and poet in New Hyde Park. He is the author of, *You Might Fall In* (Local Gems Press, 2014), *Wave into Wave, Light into Light: Poems and Places* (IPBooks.net, 2019), *When Sunset Weeps: Homage to Emily Dickinson* (David Robert Books, 2020), and *Old Caterpillar: Haiku and Senryu* (Local Gems Press, 2020).

Gloria O'lander is an optimist and poet at heart. Now that she is retired, she has the time to express her poetry through the written word. Gloria enjoys walks along the shoreline, searching for beach glass, shells and other sea treasures and listening to the music of the ocean -- one of the best ways to experience the healing powers of nature. This is her first offering of her works to the poetry world.

Tom Oleszczuk has published in NY, California, and elsewhere, and has hosted readings in Brooklyn, Manhattan, and Long Island. He lives in Sag Harbor with his wife Heidi and their 3 cats.

Sherri London Pastolove has published two poetry collections, *Cowgirls* and *Love in D Major*. Her poems have appeared in *Newsday, NCPLS Reviews, October Hill Magazine,* the *911 Memorial Artists Registry,* and most recently, *Corona: An Anthology of Poems.* You can follow her blog @ www.sherridarling.blogspot.com.

Marlene C Patti is mostly a stay at home mom to Frankie and Tommy, a guinea pig named Georgie and a wife to Daniel. She resides in Selden and emigrated from Chile in 1993. Currently she is the Chair of the Town of Brookhaven Disability Task Force and she hopes to make Brookhaven accesible and usable to people of all abilities. Find her online @marleneiskey.

Mary C. M. Phillips is a caffeinated wife, mother, writer and musician. Her works have been published in numerous bestselling inspirational anthologies. As a musician she has toured nationally with artists such as Matthew Sweet, Marti Jones & Don Dixon, Rob Bartlett, and satirist, Barry Mitchell. She recently released her first spoken-word collection, *Music of the Forest* (Rock-it Science Records). Mary blogs at caffeineepiphanies.com

Kelly Powell is a poet from Long Island. She is a graduate of SUNY Binghamton and the single mother of a transgender graduate of Stonybrook! We love state schools…she hopes you have a great day

Diana R. Richman, Ph.D. licensed psychologist, has been in private practice for many years. Listening to stories shared by souls, authoring self-help publications, writing rhymes for special occasions since childhood, and playng the cello in community orchestras evoked the desire to express her soul's voice through the musical language of poetry.

Allie Rieger is a life long resident of Suffolk County. On her down time not only does she like reading and writing, but watching horror movies with her cats. She also has the unfortunate skill of killing all her house plants.

Martin Rocek lives in Setauket on Long Island and teach theoretical physics at Stony Brook university.

Adele Seagraves Rodriguez is a life-long resident of Long Island, NY. She grew up in West Islip and currently lives in Bohemia with her husband and cat. She has been writing poetry and short stories since she was a teenager.

Rita B. Rose is an internationally published poet and author. She is also the current Long Island LGBTQ Poet Laureate as deemed by The Long Island Gay and Lesbian Film Festival (2018-21). She is also the recipient of two Bards Awards for literature (2018).

Marc Rosen spends most of his time with his nose in a book or his face at a screen. Somewhere in all of that, he sometimes manages to be productive, occasionally even writing a poem or two.

A. A. Rubin's work has appeared recently in Love Letters To Poe, Bards Annual, and Poetica. He can be reached on social media as @TheSurrealAri, or through his website, www.aarubin.com.

Christopher Santiago is a Sociocultural Anthropologist, Poet and Artist who has taught at several universities and completed years of fieldwork in Ecuador, Peru and Bolivia. He holds a Ph.D. from Columbia University, focusing on peasant resistance to transnational gold mining in Cajamarca, Peru. Exhibitions include Flowers for All Occasions, The Living Gallery, and Reckless Arts, Pari Passu, Contemporary Petite, Nth Gallery. Santiago has been an active member in the Bushwick music and arts scene for over a decade, organizing and participating in performances. He is currently a professor in the Sociology and Anthropology Department at The College of Staten Island, CUNY, and is recently published in The Psychoanalytic Review and upcoming at HAU: Journal of Ethnographic Theory. Santiago recently moved to Wassaic, NY. He grew up in East Setauket in Long Island, New York and his family is still there

Robert Savino, Suffolk County Poet Laureate 2015-2017 & Bards Laureate 2019-2021, is a native Long Island poet, Board Member at the Walt Whitman Birthplace and winner of the 2008 Oberon Poetry Prize. Robert is the co-editor of a bilingual collection of Long Island Italian Americans Poets (*No Distance Between Us*). His books include *fireballs of an illuminated scarecrow* and *Inside a Turtle Shell*. As a mentor he enjoys being the key that unlocks doors of creative minds.

Joseph E. Scalia was born in Brooklyn. He taught English and Creative Writing to reluctant high school students. He started writing his poetry on bathroom walls and eventually graduated to paper. He has written and published more than nine books and paints watercolors. (josephescalia.com)

Thea Schiller, a New York poet and psychotherapist facilitates a poetry workshop at the Somers library in Somers, N.Y. and practices psychotherapy in CT. She holds a B.A. in creative writing from The City University of New York, and an MS in counseling from Western CT State University. Her poem, "Sarah" was the Orchard Poetry Prize winner in Furrow, University of Wisconsin. Recently, she has been nominated for a Pushcart Prize and her poems have appeared in The San Diego Annual Poetry Review 2017-2018, Edify Fiction, The Ravens Perch, 4th & Sycamore, Hevria, Lucent Dreaming and The Tenth Muse as well as many small literary journals in the past. When given the chance she follows her muse from Norway to Greece.

Sophia Schiralli is an editor and teacher from Long Island. She loves to travel, and has lived in China and Brazil. Her favorite poets include Dickinson, Bukowski, and Tennyson.

Christina Schlitt is a creative writer, children's book author and photographer who has been writing poetry since her childhood. She's always been an animal/nature lover so many of her poems are nature-themed. Other frequent topics of her poetry are current events, science fiction and the meaning of life. Christina is a member of the writers'/artists' community in East Setauket where she lives with her husband Dan and her pet cats.

Karen Schulte is a retired social worker and therapist who began writing in grade school and, since retirement, has had her poetry published in a number of journals and anthologies including, Long Island Quarterly, 25th Anniversary Edition, Poetica Magazine, Paterson Review, Bards Annual, PPA Literary Review, NCPL Literary Review. Her collection of poetry, "Where Desire Settles," won first place in the Writer's Digest 2017 Annual Contest for a self-published book of poetry and recently her poem, "Displaced," won honorable mention in their national poetry contest for 2019.

Barbara Segal, poet and visual artist, is published in numerous poetry journals, including Bards Annual, Oberon, Mobius, Long Island Quarterly, The Avocet, Long Island Sounds, NCPL Society Review, and the PPA Review and PPA Haiku Annual, for which she was a first prize winner. Her first chapbook, *The Secret Road: Walking with Persephone* (Finishing Line Press) will soon be released.

Jacqueline Shortell-McSweeney writes only when inspired, or when her Muse, Noreen, stands over her with a metaphorical rolling pin. At other times, she has worked as a producer for Women Make Movies(Where WHY WOMEN STAY was produced and directed.), a video artist at Henry St., Settlement, first union woman grip on the East Coast, and then, as a lawyer, in hopes she could sue some of those responsible for her Me-Too moments in the union. Finally, as an attorney for Women's Venture Fund, Ms. Shortell-

Mcsweeney worked with women entrepreneurs to help build their businesses.

Leslie Simon is a published author, her poems have appeared in several anthologies. Recently, she published her first book, *Pieces of My Heart*. It tells her journey of depression and loss to healing and recovery. Her book is unique in that it illustrates her handmade quilts to evoke emotions of the poems.

Diane Simone-Lutz has taught writing and literature at LIU Post and other local universities for thirty years. Recently, she earned her Master's Degree in Social Work. Her poetry has been published in a number of journals, including Confrontation, The Nassau Review, and Long Island Quarterly.

Ray Simons is a born & raised Long Islander. He served with FDNY-EMS at the World Trade Center Attack. He writes mostly Poetry Therapy & was a Peer Counselor with FDNY for many years.

Vijaya Singh has called Long Island, NY home since the age of 7. Vijaya works in Healthcare/Pharma PR but is most passionate about writing and uses poetry as a therapeutic outlet. She hopes to one day publish her work.

Emily-Sue Sloane (emilysuesloane.com) lives in Huntington Station, NY. Writing helps her to appreciate life, especially in a pandemic. She finds inspiration in the backyard, at the beach, in the woods, and in watching and listening to people along the way. Her poems have appeared in various print and online journals and anthologies.

Toni-Cara Stelitano is a holistic psychotherapist, artist, and poet. She is inspired by women, their relationships with themselves, and the beauty that is born of their healing. Her private practice is in Commack, NY.

Lennon Stravato A native Long Islander, Lennon Stravato is a screenwriter, lyricist, poet, and former Foreign Policy Contributor for The Hill newspaper in Washington D.C.

Barbara Southard, Suffolk County Poet Laureate 2019-2021, has currently been partnering with Richard, Bronson, Kate Dickson, Tony Policano and Sharon Dockweiler in providing Zoom poetry workshops for the community. Books: *Remember* 2008, *Time & Space* 2020, both published by Allbook Books

Douglas G. Swezey received his B.A. in English and Art History from Stony Brook University in 2004. He has written as a journalist for many weekly newspapers and was the Managing Editor of *Government Food Services Magazine* and author of *Stony Brook University: Off The Record* (College Prowler, 2005). He currently serves on the Board of Directors for the Bard's Initiative and is the co-founder of Super Poem Sunday.

Allison Teicher-Fahrbach is the Director of Curriculum Development for Windows of Opportunity, Inc. and an educator in Queens, NY. While this twice-published author is writing and working towards education reform, she is a podcast co-host, grilled-cheese enthusiast, wife, and mother. More information about her work can be found at: https://campsite.bio/windowsofopportunity.

John Tucker A husband, father and grandfather while in retirement enjoys substitute teaching at Lawrence Woodmere Academy, yoga, hiking and attending poetry events. Published in several PPA Literary Reviews and Bards Annual 2020.

J R (Judy) Turek, 2019 Walt Whitman LI Poet of the Year, Superintendent of Poetry for the LI Fair, 2020 Hometown Hero by the *East Meadow Herald*, Bards Laureate 2013-2015, 24 years as Moderator of the Farmingdale Creative Writing Group, editor, workshop leader, author of six full-length poetry collections, 'The Purple Poet' lives on Long Island with her soul-mate husband, Paul, her dogs, and her extraordinarily extensive shoe collection. msjevus@optonline.net

Rekha Valliappan's poems and prose poems have featured in a variety of journals and magazines including Ann Arbor Review, The Sandy River Review, Nixes Mate Review, Wellington Street Review, The Pangolin Review, Red Fez, Press 53/Prime Number Magazine, Small Orange Poetry Journal, The Minison Project and other venues. A former university lecturer, her poem was nominated for the Pushcart Prize by Liquid Imagination.

Anne E. Wagenbrenner, a writer who lives in New York's Suffolk County, is currently working on a novel. Her short stories have appeared in several anthologies that are available on Amazon.com. You can find her on Twitter @Wagenbrenner1, or on Facebook at https://www.facebook.com/anne.wagenbrenner.

James P. Wagner (Ishwa) is an editor, publisher, award-winning fiction writer, essayist, historian, performance poet, and alum twice over (BA & MALS) of Dowling College. He is the publisher for Local Gems Poetry Press and the Senior Founder and President of the Bards Initiative. He is also the founder and Grand Laureate of Bards Against Hunger, a series of poetry readings and anthologies dedicated to gathering food for local pantries that operates in over a dozen states. His most recent individual collection of poetry is *Everyday Alchemy*. He was the Long Island, NY National Beat Poet Laureate from 2017-2019. He was the Walt Whitman Bicentennial Convention Chairman and teaches poetry workshops at the Walt Whitman Birthplace State Historic Site. James has edited over 100 poetry anthologies and hosted book launch events up and down the East Coast. He was named the National Beat Poet Laureate of the United States from 2020-2021. He owns and operates The Dog-Eared Bard's Book Shop in East Northport, NY.

Jillian Wagner earned her BA in Creative Writing from Dowling College. She is an active member of Fanfiction.net and is working on her collection of short stories entitled *13 Dark Tales*. She was one of the founding editors of *Conspiracy*, a genre fiction magazine at Dowling College. She is a certified paralegal and sits on the board for the Bards Initiative. She currently helps operate The Dog-Eared Bard's Book Shop.

Margarette Wahl, Special Ed Teacher Aide and Poet from Long Island. She is published in a number of Anthologies, three chapbooks with Local Gems Press. She's a Performance Poet Association cohost, member of Bards Initiative, and advisor for Nassau County Poet Laureate Society.

Herb Wahlsteen earned a B.A. in English from CA. St. U., Fullerton, and an M. A. in English from Columbia U. He then worked many years as a high-school teacher in New York City Public Schools. He was a finalist in the *Yale Series of Younger Poets* contest (1989, ***Adam and Eve in the 20th Century***, from which came the poem published here, James Merrill, judge), placed 3rd in the *Writer's Digest* 77th Annual Writing Competition: Rhyming Category, and has had poems published in local, national, and international publications.

George Wallace is writer in residence at the Walt Whitman Birthplace, first poet laureate of Suffolk County, and author of 38 chapbooks of poetry. A native of Long Island and New York City, he travels worldwide to share his poetry.

Virginia Walker, PhD, taught writing and literature courses at New England and LI colleges. She is the co-author of the poetry book *Neuron Mirror* (with Michael Walsh). Her poems have appeared in *Poets 4 Paris*, *Suffolk County Poetry Review*, *Bards Annual*, *The Light of City and Sea*, and the *Humanist*. She lives on Shelter Island.

Jack Zaffos has been writing poetry since 18 years. After retirement he made a commitment to get his work out to the public and to work seriously at composing poetry. He was the Calendar Coordinator for PPA and hopes soon to resume that role. He has three books published *Meditations Of The Heart, Songlines In The Wilderness* and *Lyrics From A Singing Stream.*

Steven Zaluski is a long Island artist and SUNY Stony Brook graduate, class of 1974. He creates metal sculpture, that is collected around the world, and loves to paint, write, create music and video, improvise performance art, swim in the ocean, bays and lakes, and enjoy life wherever he travels...

Thomas Zampino's poems have appeared in *Bard's Annual 2019, Bard's Annual 2020, Trees in a Garden of Ashes* (2020), *Otherwise Engaged* (2020 and 2021), *Chaos, A Poetry Vortex* (2020), *Nassau County Voices in Verse* (2020), twice in *Verse-Virtual* (an on-line anthology), *Silver Birch Press* and a video production of *Precise Moment* by actor Gui Agustini. His own book of poetry *Precise Moment*, was published in August 2021.

Donna Zephrine was born in Harlem New York and grew up in Bay Shore, Long island. She went to Brentwood High School, graduated from Columbia University School of Social Work in May 2017 and currently works for the New York State Office of Mental Health at Pilgrim Psychiatric Center Outpatient SOCR (State Operated Community Residence). She is a combat veteran who completed two tours in Iraq. Donna has participated in various veteran writing workshops throughout NYC. Recently Donna was featured USA Warrior stories took part in Warrior Chorus and Decruit which encourage self-expression through looking as classical literature and performing it while relating it to your own life with war and trauma. Currently

Lewis Zimmerman is a retired Science teacher. He has enjoyed poetry all his life, in addition to his other interests that include music, travel, photography and literature. He lives with his wife Joyce in East Meadow NY.

A multi-purpose poetry project, The Bards Initiative is dedicated to connecting poetry communities, while promoting the writing and performance of poetry. The Initiative provides avenues for poets to share their work and encourages the use of poetry for social change.

In addition, the Initiative aims to make use of modern technologies to help spread poetry and encourage and inspire poetry, particularly in the younger generations. It is the core belief of the Bards Initiative that poetry is the voice of the people and can be used to help create a sense of sharing and community.

www.bardsinitiative.weebly.com

Local Gems Poetry Press is a small Long Island based poetry press dedicated to spreading poetry through performance and the written word. Local Gems believes that poetry is the voice of the people, and as the sister organization of the Bards Initiative, believes that poetry can be used to make a difference.

www.localgemspoetrypress.com

Made in the USA
Middletown, DE
14 November 2021